Physical Characteristics of the American Eskimo Dog

(from the American Kennel Club's breed standard)

Body: Strong and compact, but not cobby. The chest is deep and broad with well-sprung ribs. Slight tuck-up of belly just behind the ribs. The back is straight, broad, level, and muscular. The loin is strong and well-muscled.

Tail: Set moderately high and reaches approximately to the point of hock when down. It is carried loosely on the back, although it may be dropped when at rest.

Hindquarters: Well angulated. The upper thighs are well developed. Stifles are well bent. Hock joints are well let down and firm. The rear pasterns are straight. Legs are parallel from the rear. Feet are as described for the front legs.

Size: All measurements are heights at withers: Toy, 9 inches to and including 12 inches; Miniature, over 12 inches to and including 15 inches; and Standard, over 15 inches to and including 19 inches.

Color: Pure white is the preferred color, although white with biscuit cream is permissible. The skin is pink or gray.

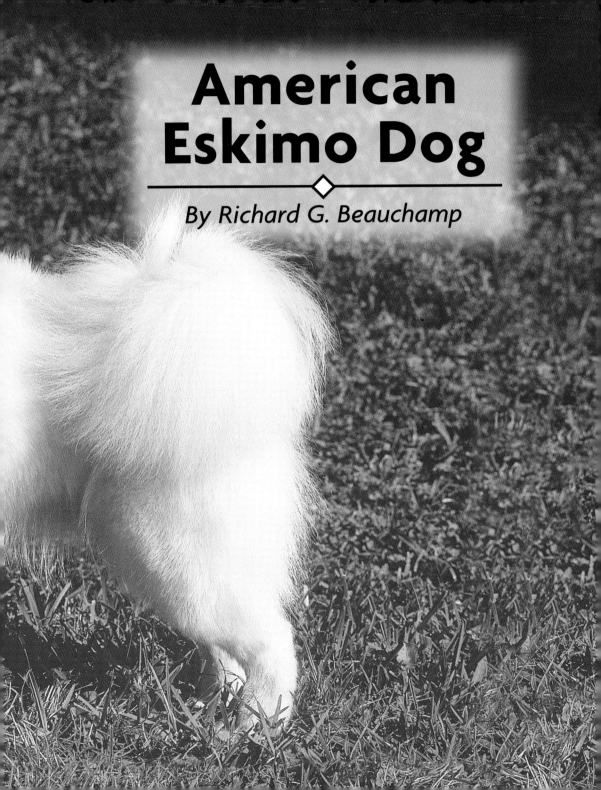

American Eskimo Dog

By Richard G. Beauchamp

Contents

KENNEL CLUB BOOKS: **AMERICAN ESKIMO DOG**
ISBN: 1-59378-353-1

Copyright © 2003 Kennel Club Books, Inc.
308 Main Street, Allenhurst, NJ 07711 USA
Cover Design Patented: US 6,435,559 B2 • Printed in South Korea

Photos by Isabelle Francais with additional photographs by:
Norvia Behling, T. J. Calhoun, Carolina Biological Supply, Doskocil, James Hayden-Yoav, James R. Hayden, RBP, Carol Ann Johnson, Bill Jonas, Dwight R. Kuhn, Dr. Dennis Kunkel, Mikki Pet Products, Phototake, Jean Claude Revy, Dr. Andrew Spielman, Alice van Kempen and R. Willbie.

The owner wishes to thank the owners of the dogs featured in this book, including Bobbi Leigh Davis, Dr. Athena Farrell/Natur Kennels, Carol Gloetzner, Lucy M. Ozalas, Cindy Richards, Wm. J. Sutera and WhiteLight American Eskimo Dogs.

Illustrations by Patricia Peters.

Racing onto the pure-bred dog scene is the American Eskimo Dog, coming to us from the frozen North. The breed's beautiful white coat, happy personality and intelligence are among the traits that have gained it a loyal following around the world.

HISTORY OF THE
AMERICAN ESKIMO DOG

EARLY ORIGINS

In the beginning, there were man and wolf—not quite enemies, not quite friends. Through the centuries, however, this relationship was to change as descendants of the original wolf stock endured great anatomical changes. As a consequence of man's intervention and manipulation over time, descendants of the wolf (*Canis lupus*) became domesticated and evolved into the dogs we know today.

Observing the sizes and shapes of many of the wolf's descendants, one would be hard-pressed to detect any of the characteristics of the original wild animal from which they descended. However, there existed a branch of the family *canid* that, because of its close proximity to its wolf ancestry, retained many of the wolf's physical characteristics.

Like their undomesticated ancestors, these dogs maintained the traits that protected them from the rugged environment of northern Europe. Weather-resistant coats protected from rain and cold. They had long, coarse

GENUS *CANIS*
Dogs and wolves are members of the genus *Canis*. Wolves are known scientifically as *Canis lupus* while dogs are known as *Canis domesticus*. Dogs and wolves are known to interbreed. The term "canine" derives from the Latin-derived word *canis*. The term "dog" has no scientific basis but has been used for thousands of years. The origin of the word "dog" has never been authoritatively ascertained.

outer coats, which shed snow and rain, and dense undercoats, which insulated against sub-zero temperatures. These coats were especially abundant around the neck and chest, thereby offering double protection for the vital organs.

The plumed tail could cover and protect the nose and mouth should the animal be forced to sleep in the snow. The small prick ears were not easily frost-bitten or frozen. The muzzle had sufficient length to warm the frigid air before it reached the lungs. The leg length was suffi-cient to keep the chest and abdomen above the snow line. These dogs carried their tails horizontally or up over their

backs, rather than trailing behind in the snow.

Skeletal remains of these early wolf descendants have been found throughout northern and central Europe, northern Asia and the Arctic regions of North America. These dogs stand as the forerunners of what now are commonly referred to as the Arctic or Nordic breeds.

This group of breeds can be divided effectually into four categories: hunting dogs (Norwegian Elkhound, Chow Chow, Karelian Bear Dog, etc.); draft dogs (Alaskan Malamute, Siberian Husky, etc.); herding dogs (Samoyed, Swedish and Finnish Lapphunds, etc.) and companion dogs (including most of the spitz-type dogs—German Spitz, Pomeranian, American Eskimo, Volpino Italiano, etc.).

One specific branch of this family was known as *Canis familiaris palustris*, or more commonly and interchangeably known as both "the dog of the lake" and "the peat bog dog." Skeletons of these spitz-type dogs, said to have existed in the late Stone Age, have been found in many places throughout northern Europe. Although their exact role in the lives of the tribes with which the dogs lived cannot be fully identified, American Eskimo author and breed historian Nancy J. Hoffman suggests that they may well have served as what we today have come to think of as guard dogs—sounding the alarm by barking when danger threatened. The alert nature, rapid vocal response and protective devotion to home and hearth of the spitz breeds certainly give credibility to this belief.

THE GERMAN SPITZ BREEDS
Although the spitz-type breeds had already become popular in Germany in the early 1500s, Count Eberhard zu Sayne is the first to have been known to refer to the dogs as "Spitz." The word *spitz* is German for "sharp point." Count zu Sayne described the dogs as having no real interest in hunting but totally dedicated to their masters and protective of all of their masters' property.

It appears that the Count had great influence in Germany in that, from his first use of the term "spitz" in 1540, the word was included not only in the German vocabulary but also in the dictionaries of that country.

The spitz-type dogs came in many sizes and many colors, with each type being identified by a separate name. They all, however, shared the same physical characteristics that had distinguished them from other types of dog for many centuries prior. Historically, dog breeds and varieties within breeds have been developed in various towns and villages of continental Europe and Great Britain quite simply due to the color and size preferences of influential individuals or due to common interests of a given area's residents. The varieties often took on the names of the towns or villages in which they were developed, and sometimes the variety's name referred to the particular duties assigned to the dogs.

The German Spitz is separated into varieties according to size. This classification was used originally in Germany and is that which is used today by the Fédération Cynologique Internationale (FCI), the governing canine authority throughout continental Europe.

The Wolfspitz is the largest of the five German Spitz breeds. It stands approximately 18 or more inches at the shoulder. The

The German Wolfspitz, the largest of the German Spitzen, seen in the characteristic wolf-gray color.

only color allowed is gray. It is believed that the American Eskimo Dog descended from this variety. The next largest is the Grossspitz, sometimes called the Giant Spitz, which stands 16 inches and above at the shoulder. Colors are white, black, brown and orange. The Mittelspitz, or Standard Spitz, is ideally 11 to 14 inches tall and can be white, black, brown, wolf gray and orange. The Kleinspitz, or Small Spitz, is bred in white, black, brown, wolf gray and orange, and measures 8.5 to 11 inches tall. Finally, the Zwergspitz, or Dwarf Spitz, can be white, black, brown, wolf gray or orange, and measures less than 8.5 inches tall.

Size and color separated the varieties in Germany, but then,

as now, they all retained the same basic look. The White Spitz enjoyed great popularity both in Germany and even more so abroad. By the 1700s, the popular dog of British society was called simply the White Spitz. These dogs were particular favorites of Queen Charlotte, who was born in Germany and remembered the dogs from her childhood.

Queen Charlotte's dogs were obtained from the area around Pomerania, which had a far-reaching reputation for the excellence of its white dogs. Charlotte's treasured White Spitz came to be called the "Pomeranian" in England. This name was attributed to her creation, but no breed has ever been known by this name in Germany.

A group of German Kleinspitz, showing off some of the breed's color possibilities.

These Pomeranians gained tremendous popularity, even among England's commoners in the 1800s. The dogs weighed about 20 to 30 pounds and were said to be about 18 inches high at the shoulder. The size and color, incidentally, coincide approximately with those of the Standard variety of today's American Eskimo Dog. Shortly we will see that the Miniature variety of the Eskie seems more apt to be tied to the Pomeranian as we know it today.

It would be Queen Victoria, however, who was to have the most profound and long-lasting influence on the character of what was referred to as the Pomeranian. After ascending to the British throne, Victoria and her entourage journeyed to Italy. In Florence, she came upon a

The Pomeranian is a close relative of the Eskie.

red sable spitz that weighed only 12 pounds. She became enchanted by the little dog and brought him back to Great Britain with her. She called him Marco and he became her constant companion.

Victoria exhibited him at dog shows in London as a Pomeranian, even though he looked nothing like the larger white dogs that carried that name. Little Marco created a minor sensation, launching a demand for Pomeranians of his size and color. For a time, both the larger white and smaller colored dogs were shown simultaneously. Eventually, the smaller dogs gained such a foothold that the white dogs that had carried the name Pomeranian fell from favor and disappeared completely from the show scene. From that point on, the diminutive variety retained the name Pomeranian.

ARRIVAL AND ESTABLISHMENT IN AMERICA

Some of the larger white dogs had found their way to America by the turn of the 20th century and maintained some popularity under the name "Spitz." They no doubt emigrated to the US with the early German settlers. Unfortunately, a good many of these early dogs were somewhat sharp in temperament and were not considered entirely trustworthy.

Early in the 1900s, Mr. and Mrs. James Hall became deeply involved in breeding the White Spitz, or what was popularly known at the time as the "American Spitz." The Halls contacted the United Kennel Club (UKC) in 1913 and negotiated to have their dogs registered with that organization.

The UKC had been founded by Chauncey Z. Bennett in 1898, just a few years after the AKC had opened its doors, and was primarily a registering source for working dogs. Why the Halls chose the UKC as the breed's registering body has never been revealed, and how the breed became known as the American Eskimo Dog remains controversial. Some believe it was simply because the Halls did not like the German word *spitz*. They therefore opted for the name of their own kennel, which was "American Eskimo." This name did in fact somewhat describe the breeds used by the Eskimos of the Arctic regions, but in reality had absolutely nothing to do with the spitz dogs that the Halls were breeding.

Considering the world's political situation at the time that the Halls applied for recognition of the breed, there is another story told that may well be closer to the truth. American sentiments were dramatically anti-German at the time and, in fact, German Shepherds were referred to as Alsatians and Dachshunds as Badger Dogs. The American public wanted absolutely nothing to do with Germany or anything associated with that country. Certainly

Thomas Gainsborough (1727-1788) painted "Pomeranian and Puppy" more than 250 years ago. The breed has changed considerably since then, but its relationship to the Eskie is very obvious.

"American Eskimo" was a far more patriotic-sounding name than "German Spitz."

The first known breed standard for the American Eskimo Dog is said to have been drafted by Dr. E. G. Fuhrman, who was then-president of the UKC. Although it basically described the breed as we know it today, his draft contained some significant errors. The most important incorrect statement made was that the Eskie was a miniaturized version of the Samoyed that had been painstakingly bred down in size through the years.

From 1913, when the UKC first admitted the breed to its stud books, until 1970, the UKC accepted "single-dog registrations." That is, a dog of obvious pure breeding could be registered without benefit of a pedigree. However, the stud books of the United Kennel Club have been closed to single-dog registrations of the American Eskimo Dog since 1970. While the single-dog registry may seem unusual, many kennel clubs of the world have resorted to the same procedure. When trying to establish foundation stock for a new breed or particularly to re-establish a breed decimated by war or genetic problems, this method has been resorted to in Europe and also in Great Britain.

The American Kennel Club resorted to this same method as recently as the end of the 20th century as a response to the request of American Basenji breeders, who needed an outcross to assist them in correcting genetic problems rampant in the breed. The Basenji parent club was permitted to single-register Basenjis that had been found in the tribal villages of Africa.

SPITZ BREED NAMES

The word *spitz* actually became an umbrella term in Germany in that some of the spitz-type dogs were named in respect to the area from which they came. For instance, the Mannheimer Spitz was developed in the area of Mannheim, Germany. Other varieties were given their names because of the work they performed. The dogs that worked as guardians for the wine-growers of Germany became known as the Weinberg or Vineyard Spitz.

German Kleinspitz.

According to Nancy Hoffman and Cathy J. Flamholtz's *The American Eskimo*, 43 fanciers from across the country gathered in DeSota, Missouri in November of 1969 to form the National American Eskimo Dog Association. Thomas Maxwell was elected president of the new organization. He became one of the breed's staunchest supporters and remained in office for many years.

Mr. Maxwell's female Standard Eskie, Maxwell's Gidget, became the first UKC champion in the breed. Another dog of his breeding, Maxwell's Zsa Zsa, was to become the first Miniature champion. Many champions were bred by Mr. and Mrs. Maxwell and the couple traveled extensively, showing and winning with their dogs throughout the US.

As the years progressed and the American Eskimo grew from strength to strength, many of the breed's supporters felt that the breed deserved to be included among those breeds recognized by the American Kennel Club. In order to support their efforts in that direction, fanciers met with Carolyn Jester in 1985 to form the American Eskimo Dog Club of America (AEDCA). Carolyn Jester was named president and stud book registrar of the new organization. She served as president until 1998

STONEHENGE ON THE SPITZ

J. H. Walsh, the English author who wrote under the pseudonym "Stonehenge" in the 1800s, is regarded as an eminent dog authority and historian to this day. In his book, *Dogs of Great Britain, America and Other Countries*, he wrote about the Pomeranian or Spitz dogs in this manner: "...he is always cheerful in the house, generally free from smell either of coat or breath, and readily taught to be cleanly in all his habits. He has not the fondness for game generally exhibited by the colley, and on that account is more suited to be a ladies' pet, nor is he so pugnacious as that dog..."

The American Eskimo derives from dogs that came to us under the name White Spitz.

until July 1, 1995, at which time the Eskie attained full breed recognition as a member of the Non-Sporting Group. The American Eskimo Dog Club of America was officially recognized by the AKC as the breed's parent club.

An immediate flurry of activity arose after the date on which the breed was given full recognition, as exhibitors rushed to try their wings under AKC judges. It took only 22 days for Sandy Tocco's Stevens' Gorbachev to become the first entry in the breed's AKC record book. Gorbachev became the first AKC champion of record on July 23, 1995 at the Burbank Kennel Club show in Burbank, California.

On the first day that the breed was eligible to be shown and maintained the AEDCA stud book from its inception to its final preparation and turnover to the AKC in the fall of 1993.

On April 13, 1993, the Board of Directors of the American Kennel Club voted to accept the American Eskimo Dog into its stud book and over 1,750 dogs were registered as foundation stock. The breed was shown in the Miscellaneous Class at American Kennel Club shows

THE WHITE SPITZ

It is a known fact that there were very good representatives of the White Spitz breed in America as early as the late 1800s. At that time, British authors made reference to the fact that high-quality specimens of the breed had been imported into England from America by British citizens who had traveled to America and back. In 1919, *National Geographic* magazine carried an article that spoke of this spitz breed as having been popular "thirty or forty years ago. . .in this country."

A wintry portrait that reminds us of the American Eskimo's beginnings.

HOME SWEET HOME

One of the most highly prized characteristics of Germany's "Spitzhunds," precursors of the American Eskimo, was their lack of interest in chasing game or straying away from the home. This made the dogs ideal home guardians and they soon became the cherished breed of the common man, guarding home and hearth. The dogs were especially held in high regard by the mothers of the family, who knew that the alarm would be sounded if anyone attempted to approach the children or if the children attempted to wander off.

at an AKC show, Sierra's Orion, bred by Joe and Diana Allen and owned by C. Anne Bishop, PhD., made breed history by winning his way to first place in the Non-Sporting Group. Orion's ensuing show record proved that his first win was not serendipitous—he went on to win the first National Specialty Show of the AEDCA in February of the following year and became the first of the breed to win an all-breed Best in Show. The historic occasion took place at the Greater Emporia Kennel Club, Emporia, Kansas, in May of 1996.

The breed's accomplishments did not end in the conformation ring, as many Eskies quickly proved themselves as obedience winners. The first High in Trial and Obedience Hall of Fame titleholder was Donna J. Blews' brilliant female, Northern Lights Calah, UD, ASCA-CDX, TDI, TT, CGC.

Today, chapters of both the National American Eskimo Dog Association and the American Eskimo Dog Club exist throughout the United States. Shows are held throughout the country on almost every weekend of the year, with the NAEDA abiding by the UKC's rules and breed standards, and the AEDCA abiding by those of the AKC.

It is to the credit of the breeders and members of these organizations that great care has been taken in the placement of Eskie breeding stock and companion stock. Devoted fanciers have avoided making the American Eskimo the dog *du jour*, as witnessed by the modest numbers registered with the AKC each year. For example, at the close of 1999, the 491 individual Eskies registered by the AKC put the breed in 98th place among the 147 breeds recognized by that organization. It is also to the credit of the Eskie fancy that such great strides have been made in stabilizing and improving the breed's temperament that it is now considered to be among one of the finest home companions available.

CHARACTERISTICS OF THE
AMERICAN ESKIMO DOG

BEFORE YOU BUY

American Eskimo puppies are extremely hard to resist, so if you haven't fully decided on whether or not you should add an Eskie to your family, I would strongly suggest staying as far away as possible from visiting a breeder who has a litter. Leaving without one of these little cotton balls will be next to impossible!

It is for this very reason that the person anticipating owning an Eskie should give serious thought to his final decision. All puppies are picture-postcard cuddly and cute—Eskie puppies particularly so. There is nothing more seductive than a litter of puppies at play or these bits of white fluff nestled together sound asleep, one on top of the other. But, in addition to being cute, puppies are living, breathing and very mischievous little creatures, and they are entirely dependent upon their human owners for everything once they leave their mother and littermates.

Buying a dog, especially a puppy, before you are absolutely sure that you want to make that commitment can be a serious

WHAT'S YOUR SIZE?

The American Eskimo comes in sizes that can suit nearly every living condition, from the tiniest apartment to the country estate or farm. The sizes are: Toy, standing from 9 inches up to and including 12 inches; Miniature, standing over 12 inches up to and including 15 inches; and Standard, standing over 15 inches up to and including 19 inches. The conformation requirements for all three varieties are exactly the same, only the size differences distinguish the varieties. Which size is best for the prospective owner depends entirely upon the personal likes and circumstances of the owner.

Underneath the fluffy white coat is an abundance of agility and versatility. This Eskie enjoys an occasional lap in his family's pool.

mistake. Dog owners can be extremely enthusiastic about their respective breeds and may want to recommend them to everyone. However, the prospective owner must clearly understand the amount of time and work involved in the ownership of any dog, and he must particularly understand the character and requirements of the breed that he is considering. Failure to understand the extent of the commitment that dog ownership involves is one of the primary reasons that so many unwanted canines end their lives in animal shelters.

Before anyone contemplates the purchase of any dog, there are some very basic conditions that must be considered. One of the first important questions that must be answered is whether or not the person who will ultimately be responsible for the dog's everyday care and well-being actually wants a dog. All too often, the responsibility of the family dog's day-to-day care tends to fall on one person, usually a parent. While the children in the family may be wildly enthusiastic about having a dog, it must be remembered that they are away most of the day at school, extra-curricular activities and the like. It is often Mom or Dad who will be taking on the additional responsibility of primary care-giver for the dog.

Pets are a wonderful method of teaching responsibility to children, but it should be remembered that the enthusiasm that inspires children to promise anything in order to have a new puppy may quickly wane. Who will take care of the puppy once the novelty wears off? Does that person want a dog?

Desire to own a dog aside, does the lifestyle of the family actually provide for responsible dog ownership? If the entire

ATHLETIC ESKIE
The American Eskimo stands among the most athletic of the smaller breeds. All three sizes consistently prove that competitive events like agility and flyball come as second nature. It is important, however, always to remember that the Eskie needs patience, understanding and a gentle touch in all of his training experiences. If your Eskie senses that you lack enthusiasm in what you are trying to convey, you will be hard-pressed to convince him that what you're doing is "fun."

family is away from early morning to late at night, who will provide for all of a puppy's needs? Feeding, exercise, outdoor access and the like cannot be provided if no one is home.

Another important factor to consider is whether or not the breed of dog is suitable for the person or family with which it will be living. Considering the American Eskimo Dog gives the prospective owner several options in that the breed comes in three varieties or sizes: Standard, Miniature and Toy. A full-grown Standard-sized Eskie can handle the rough-and-tumble play of young children. A very young Toy-sized Eskie cannot.

Then, too, there is the matter of hair. A luxuriously coated dog is certainly beautiful to behold, but all of that hair takes a great deal of care. Brushing an adult Eskie requires time and patience. All long-haired dogs shed their coats in the home. Naturally, the longer the hair, the more noticeable it will be on clothing, furniture and the like.

As great as claims are for any breed's intelligence and trainability, remember that the new dog must be taught every household rule that he is to observe. Some dogs catch on more quickly than others, and puppies are just as inclined to forget or disregard lessons as young human children.

DOGS, DOGS, GOOD FOR YOUR HEART!

People usually purchase dogs for companionship, but studies show that dogs can help to improve their owners' health and level of activity, as well as lower a human's risk of coronary heart disease. Without even realizing it, when a person puts time into exercising, grooming and feeding a dog, he also puts more time into his own personal health care. Dog owners establish more routine schedules for their dogs to follow, which can have positive effects on their own health. Dogs also teach us patience, offer unconditional love and provide the joy of having a furry friend to pet!

WHY A PURE-BRED DOG?

Most dog lovers agree that all puppies are cute. Not all puppies grow up to be particularly attractive adults. Of course, this is subjective; what is considered beauty to one person is not necessarily seen as attractive to another. It is almost impossible to determine what a mixed-breed puppy will look like as an adult. It also will not be possible to determine if the mixed-breed puppy's temperament is suitable for the person or family who wishes to own him. If the puppy grows up to be too big, too hairy or too active for the owner, what then will happen to him?

Size and temperament can vary to a degree, even within pure-bred dogs. Still, selective breeding over many generations has produced dogs that give the would-be owner reasonable assurance of what the pure-bred puppy will look and act like as an adult. Esthetics completely aside, this predictability of personality is more important than one might think.

Pure-bred puppies will grow up to look like their adult relatives and, by and large, they will behave much like the rest of their family. Any dog, mixed breed or not, has the potential to be a loving companion. However, the predictability of a pure-bred dog means that, most likely, the dog will suit not only the owner's lifestyle but also that person's esthetic preferences.

Before you bring an Eskie into your household, visit breeders and spend as much time with both puppies and adults as you can. Puppies are only puppies for a short time, so be sure that the adult Eskie is the dog that appeals to you both esthetically and temperamentally.

WHO SHOULD OWN AN ESKIE?

The American Eskimo Dog is long-haired and all white—really quite beautiful. Remember, though, that the breed only looks

SHY GUYS

The Miniature and Toy varieties of some American Eskimo bloodlines produce individuals that can become so extremely devoted to their owners and families that they need extra work to keep them well socialized and friendly. With proper exposure and socialization, a well-bred Miniature or Toy Eskie can be just as outgoing as his Standard relative. It should be remembered that no breeder can absolutely guarantee the mature size of an American Eskimo purchased as a very young puppy. Some breeders are better able to predict size in that they have a long-established line made up almost exclusively of individuals of a particular size.

beautiful with care and maintenance. Don't forget that your Eskie's coat requires your attention. Although many valid claims are made for the easy care of the Eskie's coat, he still is a heavily coated white dog, and he does shed. If you appreciate the look of the breed, do realize that it will take some time and effort on your part to kept your dog looking that way.

While the Eskie can be an ideal choice for the person with allergy problems, it must be remembered that the breed, like many all-white and pink-skinned dogs, can be extremely sensitive to fleas. Unless carefully controlled, flea bites can and will lead to severe scratching. Incessant scratching results in skin eruptions and "hot spots," which are accompanied by hair loss.

The Eskie is as smart as a whip and is capable of learning just about everything that you will teach him. Your Eskie will be totally and completely dedicated to you, and that dedication must be rewarded in kind. But just because the Eskie is totally dedicated to you, do not think for a moment that you will have a dog that obeys without question. An Eskie needs a "pack leader." The breed is most secure when it is given boundaries and when the boundaries are consistently enforced.

Your Eskie must start under-

standing the household rules from the first moment he comes into your home. What it will take to accomplish this is patience, dedication and a firm but gentle hand.

Someone who needs a dog that does well living outdoors with minimal owner interaction should, in all fairness, look to another breed, or perhaps no dog at all! The Eskie must have constant human companionship and social interaction not only with his owner but also with all kinds of people and other dogs. The Eskie raised without this socialization can easily become introverted and difficult to handle.

The young American Eskimo can pass through an adolescent stage during which he decides that his owner or family is all that

Gentle but firm guidance from the beginning encourages good behavior and builds your Eskie's confidence to help him through his adolescent stage.

is necessary to his well-being. Without the benefit of social-ization, the youngster can become very anti-social unless made to understand that this behavior is unacceptable. It is up to the caring owner to help guide the Eskie through this difficult stage. Patience, persistence and support will help your Eskie through this awkward time, but it does take time and commit-ment to stay out there with the "bashful" youngster.

If you are willing to make the necessary commitment that an Eskie requires, let me assure you there are few breeds that are more versatile, devoted and adaptable. Do not forget the Eskie heritage—devoted companion and loyal protector of his human family and their household.

KEEP HIM BUSY

The American Eskimo Dog has a very high intelligence and trainability level. This can prove to be both an asset and a liability. The Eskie whose schoolwork is neglected can become a destructive and noisy nuisance. An Eskie has to put all of that brain power to good use somewhere, and if his owner doesn't show him how and where, the Eskie can come up with ideas that may absolutely astonish his owner...and not necessarily in a good way!

PERSONALITY PLUS

This is not a breed to be relegated to kennel life or an outdoor run, with only occasional access to your life and environment. The very essence of the Eskie is in his personality and devoted nature, which are best developed by constant human contact. Whether a favorite of the the royal families or a circus performer, everything the Eskie has done has been done in the company of his human family. Historically, the American Eskimo Dog has always been a close companion to man. The breed is happiest and best able to fully develop its many admirable characteristics when allowed to continue that association.

The Eskie owner must be prepared for the fact that the breed is intent upon protecting his home and his human family from any impending danger or harm. The best way that an Eskie can do this is to warn you when he perceives the possibility of anything threatening the safety of you and your family. This is accomplished by barking—sounding the alarm to give you a warning.

Barking is a characteristic typical of all of the spitz breeds, and no less so of the American Eskimo. It is important for your Eskie to learn the difference between necessary and unneces-sary barking. The latter can be nerve-wracking to an owner and a nuisance to neighbors. Eskies are smart dogs and will quickly learn barking boundaries if strictly enforced. Do remember, however, that the warning bark is a part of the Eskie's heritage. It is up to the owner to make sure that his Eskie understands when and where barking is appropriate.

We are never surprised to hear that an Eskie that has been completely housebroken will suddenly forget all of his manners or will become destructive in protest of being left alone too often or for too long. Some Eskies will let their owners know that they are not getting the attention they need by destroying house-hold items, particularly those things that belong to the individ-ual whom the dog particularly misses.

This does not mean that you must be home all day long to hold your Eskie's paw and cater to his whims. Many Eskies are owned by working people who are away for a good part of the day. Their dogs are well mannered and trust-worthy when left home alone.

The key here is the quality rather than quantity of the time spent with an Eskie. Morning or evening walks, grooming sessions, regular training routines and consistent rule enforcement are vital to the breed's personality development and attitude. If you are away for most of the day, be sure to include your Eskie in your

life when you are at home. Eskies live to be talked to and praised by their owners.

Everything about the Eskie's personality indicates that it is a non-aggressive breed. At the same time, though, the breed has an inherent wariness of strangers. We cannot simply dismiss the breed's history because we don't feel we need protection. An Eskie's heritage and original role is that of household guardian. Still, it would be totally out of character for an Eskie to challenge his owner on any point, regardless of how much he might object to what he is being asked to do.

This is not to say that an American Eskimo is beyond test-ing your patience or the reality of

A mutually beneficial way for the Eskie to expend some energy is in activities done with his owner.

the boundaries you set. The Eskie can be very headstrong and may well act as though he has not heard your command. In situations like this, it may be necessary for you to sit your Eskie down, taking hold of the scruff of his neck with both hands and looking him in the eye, and to repeat your command. A stern and disapproving voice, and consistency in enforcing the rules, are usually more than sufficient to let an American Eskimo know that you disapprove of what he is doing. It is never necessary to strike your Eskie in any circumstance. A sharp "No!" is normally more than it takes to make your point.

The Eskie makes a great effort to please his owner and is highly trainable as long as the trainer is not heavy-handed. Any training problems encountered are far more apt to be due to the owner rather than to the Eskie's lack of understanding or inability to learn.

Do not make the mistake of some Eskie owners, who think of their canine companions as "little people." They spoil their dogs to the point where, instead of being additions to the household, the dogs become nothing but nuisances. It must be understood that the American Eskimo is first and foremost a *dog*. Dogs, like their ancestor, the wolf, are pack animals in need of a pack

leader. Your Eskie is dependent upon you to provide that leadership. When that leadership is not provided, an Eskie can easily become confused and neurotic.

Setting boundaries is important to your Eskie's well-being and to his relationship with you. As we mentioned earlier, the American Eskimo Dog is not vindictive or stubborn if properly trained, but the breed does need guidance in order to achieve its potential.

MALE OR FEMALE?
In many breeds, differences between the sexes are important considerations that often influence the prospective owner's choice of a puppy. Of course, there are sex-related differences in the American Eskimo that the prospective buyer should consider. In the end, however, the assets and liabilities of each sex

> **TAKING CARE**
> Science is showing that as people take care of their pets, the pets are taking care of their owners. A recent study published in the *American Journal of Cardiology* found that having a pet can prolong his owner's life. Pet owners generally have lower blood pressure, and pets help their owners to relax and keep more physically fit. It was also found that pets help to keep the elderly connected to their communities.

do balance each other out and the final choice remains with individual preference.

The male Eskie makes just as loving, devoted and trainable companion as the female, but in some cases he can be a bit more headstrong as an adolescent. Here again, the owner's dedication to establishing and maintaining discipline will determine the final outcome.

There is one important point to consider in determining your choice between male and female. While both must be trained not to relieve themselves in the home, the male has a natural instinct to lift his leg and urinate to mark his home territory. This may sound confusing to many dog owners, but a male's marking his home turf has absolutely nothing to do with whether or not the dog is housebroken. The two responses come from entirely different needs and must be dealt with in that manner. Some dogs are more difficult to train not to mark within the confines of the household than others. Males that are used for breeding are more prone to this response and are even harder to break of doing so.

On the other hand, females have their semi-annual heat cycles (estruses) once they have reached sexual maturity. In the case of the female American Eskimo, this occurs for the first time at about six to nine months of age. These

DO YOU WANT TO LIVE LONGER?
If you like to volunteer, it is wonderful if you can take your dog to a nursing home once a week for several hours. The elder community loves to have a dog with which to visit, and often your dog will bring a bit of companionship to someone who is lonely or somewhat detached from the world. You will be not only bringing happiness to someone else but also keeping your dog busy—and we haven't even mentioned the fact that it has been discovered that volunteering helps to increase your own longevity!

cycles are accompanied by a bloody vaginal discharge that creates the need to confine the female so that she does not soil her surroundings. The need for confining the female in heat is especially important to prevent her becoming pregnant by some neighborhood Lothario. It must be understood that the female has no control over this bloody discharge, so it has nothing to do with training.

Both of these sexually related problems can be eliminated by spaying the female and neutering the male. Unless an Eskie is purchased expressly for breeding or showing from a breeder capable of making this judgment, your pet should be sexually altered. Ethical breeders will include a spay/neuter clause in sales agreements for puppies that will not be used

> **WHO'S THERE?**
> The average Eskie is more inclined to "tolerate" strangers than he is to rush out and invite them into your home. He is instinctively territorial and knows that his job is to keep a watchful eye on you and yours. Therefore, someone your Eskie knows nothing about could pose a problem in his eyes, and he will be inclined to wait and see rather than roll out the welcome wagon right away.

for showing or breeding, but will be kept solely as pets and companions.

It should be understood, however, that spaying and neutering are not reversible procedures. Spayed females or neutered males are not allowed to be shown in conformation shows in most countries, and altered animals will never be able to be used for breeding.

There is a difference in the amount of coat carried by the male and female American Eskimo. The male Eskie normally carries a much heavier coat than the female, so there is more for the male to shed during the annual springtime coat casting. On the other hand, the semi-annual heat cycles of the female are also accompanied by shedding. Thus, while there is a bit less hair to be shed by the female, it happens twice as often in unspayed bitches.

The ever-alert Eskie, in keeping with his spitz ancestry, keeps a vigilant watch over his and his owners' territory.

BREED STANDARD FOR THE

AMERICAN ESKIMO DOG

INTRODUCTION TO THE BREED STANDARD

While the AKC and UKC breed standards do differ slightly, what they both attempt to describe is basically the same dog. The American Eskimo Dog is, and must always remain, a serviceable and healthy dog, free of exaggerations of any kind and ideally suited as a companion to man.

Like its undomesticated ancestors, the American Eskimo Dog retains those characteristics that would theoretically allow the breed to survive in the wild should the necessity arise. The breed has no gross exaggerations or incapacitating anatomical characteristics.

The proper coat of the Eskie protects the breed from both the sub-zero temperatures of winter and the scalding temperatures of summer. As already mentioned, the longer, coarse outer coat helps shed both rain and snow, while the short, dense undercoat insulates against both heat and cold. The especially profuse coat around the neck and chest is designed to provide extra protection for those areas. The heavily coated plumed tail protects the dog's nose and mouth in cold temperatures and snow; the tail covers the face when the dog curls up. When in motion, the tail is carried over the back so that is does not trail behind in the snow or become caught up in brambles or undergrowth.

The coat should be white, but shadings of biscuit and cream are allowed. No other color is permitted. Important points are pigmentation and eye color. Eye rims, nose and lips should be dark; the darker the better. Also, blue eyes are totally unacceptable; eyes should be dark to medium brown.

The Eskie's balanced construction makes him an all-around canine athlete, both powerful and agile—bearing comparison to the human decathlon champion. The well-conditioned Eskie is muscular and fit with little excess to hinder his quick and easy movement. The breed is slender enough to manipulate over, under, around and through.

What the standards ask for in the way of construction and balance applies to all three varieties of the breed—Toy,

Miniature and Standard. While the Toy and Miniature varieties may never be asked to survive in the wild, it must be remembered that they are simply a miniaturization of the Standard variety and that all aspects of type, balance and soundness apply. The UKC breed standard does not recognize the Toy variety. The standards of both the AKC and UKC are presented here for comparative purposes.

THE AMERICAN KENNEL CLUB STANDARD FOR THE AMERICAN ESKIMO DOG

General Appearance: The American Eskimo Dog, a loving companion dog, presents a picture of strength and agility, alertness and beauty. It is a small to medium-size Nordic type dog, always white, or white with biscuit cream. The American Eskimo Dog is compactly built and well balanced, with good substance, and an alert, smooth gait. The face is Nordic type with erect triangular shaped ears, and distinctive black points (lips, nose, and eye rims). The white double coat consists of a short, dense undercoat, with a longer guard hair growing through it forming the outer coat, which is straight with no curl or wave. The coat is thicker and longer around the neck and chest forming a lion-like ruff, which is more noticeable on dogs than on bitches. The rump and hind legs down to the hocks are also covered with thicker, longer hair forming the characteristic breeches. The richly plumed tail is carried loosely on the back.

Size, Proportion, Substance: *Size:* There are three separate size divisions of the American Eskimo Dog (all measurements are heights at withers): Toy, 9 inches to and including 12 inches; Miniature, over 12 inches to and including 15 inches; and Standard, over 15 inches to and including 19 inches. There is no preference for size within each division. *Disqualification:* Under 9 inches or over 19 inches. *Proportion:* Length of back from point of shoulder to point of buttocks is slightly greater than height at withers, an approximate 1.1 to 1 ratio. *Substance:* The American Eskimo Dog is strong and compactly built with adequate bone.

Head: *Expression* is keen, intelligent, and alert. *Eyes* are not fully round, but slightly oval. They should be set well apart, and not slanted, prominent or bulging. Tear stain, unless severe, is not to be faulted. Presence of tear stain should not outweigh consideration of type, structure, or temperament. Dark to medium brown is the preferred eye color. Eye rims are black to dark brown. Eyelashes are white. *Faults:* Amber eye color or pink eye rims. *Disqualification:* Blue eyes. *Ears* should conform to head size and be triangular, slightly blunt-tipped, held erect, set on high yet well apart, and blend softly with the head. *Skull* is slightly crowned and softly wedge-shaped, with widest breadth between the ears. The stop is well defined, although not abrupt. The *muzzle* is broad, with length not exceeding the length of the skull, although it may be slightly shorter. *Nose* pigment is black to dark brown. *Lips* are thin and tight, black to dark brown in color. *Faults:* Pink nose pigment or pink lip pigment. The *jaw* should be strong with a full complement of close fitting teeth. The *bite* is scissors or pincer.

Neck, Topline, Body: The *neck* is carried proudly erect, well set on, medium in length, and in a strong, graceful arch. The *topline* is level. The *body* of the American Eskimo Dog is strong and compact, but not cobby. The chest is deep and broad with well-sprung ribs. Depth of chest extends approximately to point of elbows. Slight tuck-up of belly just behind the ribs. The back is straight, broad, level, and muscular. The loin is strong and well-muscled. The American Eskimo Dog is neither too long nor too short coupled. The *tail* is set moderately high and reaches approximately to the

point of hock when down. It is carried loosely on the back, although it may be dropped when at rest.

American Eskimo Dog in profile, showing correct type, balance and structure.

Forequarters: Forequarters are well angulated. The shoulder is firmly set and has adequate muscle but is not overdeveloped. The shoulder blades are well laid back and slant 45° with the horizontal. At the point of shoulder the shoulder blade forms an approximate right angle with the upper arm. The legs are parallel and straight to the pasterns. The pasterns are strong and flexible with a slant of about 20°. Length of leg in proportion to the body. Dewclaws on the front legs may be removed at the owner's discretion; if present, they are not to be

faulted. Feet are oval, compact, tightly knit and well padded with hair. Toes are well arched. Pads are black to dark brown, tough and deeply cushioned. Toenails are white.

Hindquarters: Hindquarters are well angulated. The lay of the pelvis is approximately 30° to the horizontal. The upper thighs are well developed. Stifles are well bent. Hock joints are well let down and firm. The rear pasterns are straight. Legs are parallel from the rear and turn neither in nor out. Feet are as described for the front legs. Dewclaws are not present on the hind legs.

Coat: The American Eskimo Dog has a stand-off double coat consisting of a dense undercoat and a longer coat of guard hair growing through it to form the outer coat. It is straight with no curl or wave. There is a pronounced ruff around the neck which is more noticeable on dogs than bitches. Outer part of the ear should be well covered with short, smooth hair, with longer tufts of hair growing in front of ear openings. Hair on muzzle should be short and smooth. The backs of the front legs should be well feathered, as are the rear legs down to the hock. The tail is covered profusely with long hair. *There is to be no trimming of the whiskers or body coat and such trimming will be severely penalized.* The only permissible trimming is to neaten the feet and the backs of the rear pasterns.

Color: Pure white is the preferred color, although white with biscuit cream is permissible. Presence of biscuit cream should not outweigh consideration of type, structure, or temperament. The skin of the American Eskimo Dog is pink or gray. *Disqualification:* Any color other than white or biscuit cream.

Gait: The American Eskimo Dog shall trot, not pace. The gait is agile, bold, well balanced, and frictionless, with good forequarter reach and good hindquarter drive. As speed increases, the American Eskimo Dog will single track with the legs converging toward the center line of gravity while the back remains firm, strong, and level.

Temperament: The American Eskimo Dog is intelligent, alert, and friendly, although slightly conservative. It is never overly shy nor aggressive, and such dogs are to be severely penalized in the show ring. At home it is an excellent watchdog, sounding a warning bark to announce the arrival of any stranger. It is protective of its home and family, although it does not threaten to bite or attack people. The American Eskimo Dog learns new tasks quickly and is eager to please.

Disqualifications:
Any color other than white or biscuit cream
Blue eyes
Height: under 9 or over 19 inches.

Approved: October 11, 1994
Effective: November 30, 1994

THE UNITED KENNEL CLUB STANDARD FOR THE AMERICAN ESKIMO DOG

Revised April 1, 1999

History: The American Eskimo is a member of the ancient and wide-ranging Spitz family of dogs. One 18th-century German historian claimed that the Spitz was the ancestor of all domestic breeds. White Spitzes were popular in Pomerania and in the coastal regions of Germany. Sailors traded the white dogs throughout Europe. When Queen Charlotte of England acquired several white Spitzes, the dogs became fashionable among British aristocrats. White Spitzes appear in several Gainsborough paintings.

German immigrants probably brought the white Spitz dogs to the United States, where they served as watchdogs, family pets, and circus dogs.

Known as the German Spitz in its homeland, the breed was renamed the American Eskimo in 1917. This was probably a reaction to the unpopularity during World War I of anything associated with Germany.

The American Eskimo was recognized by the United Kennel Club in 1913.

General Appearance: The American Eskimo is a well balanced, typical model of a working type Spitz dog, ranging in size from 11 to 19 inches. The body is well balanced and proportioned, appearing neither clumsy nor racy. The length of back from withers to set-on of tail is equal to the height from withers to the ground. The head is wedge-shaped, with erect triangular ears, and readily distinguished black points (nose, lips, and eye rims). The American Eskimo has a thick, white double coat. The chest, neck, and forepart of the shoulders are typically covered with a lion-like mane. The backs of the forelegs are well

are typically more profuse on males than females. The tail is richly plumed and carried over the back. With its alert, smooth carriage, the American Eskimo presents a picture of natural beauty, alertness, strength, and agility.

Characteristics: The American Eskimo is intelligent, alert, and energetic. This breed is loyal and friendly, but can be conservative with strangers. Overly aggressive or overly shy dogs are penalized.

Head: Head size conforms proportionately to body size. The wedge-shaped head denotes power. The stop is well defined, but not abrupt.

   Skull—The skull is broad and slightly crowned.

   Muzzle—The muzzle conforms proportionately to head size and is covered with short, smooth hair. The jaws are strong. Lips are tight and black to dark brown in color. *Faults:* Saggy flews; unpigmented lips.

   Teeth—A full complement of sound, white teeth that meet in a scissors bite is preferred. A level bite is permissible. *Faults:* Overshot or undershot bite.

   Nose—The nose leather is black to dark brown. *Fault:* Absence of dark pigment.

   Eyes—The eyes are medium, oval in shape but not slanted. Eyes are dark to medium brown

BREEDING CONSIDERATIONS

The decision to breed your dog is one that must be considered carefully and researched thoroughly before moving into action. Some people believe that breeding will make their bitches happier or that it is an easy way to make money. Unfortunately, indiscriminate breeding only worsens the rampant problem of pet overpopulation, as well as putting a considerable dent in your pocketbook. As for the bitch, the entire process from mating through whelping is not an easy one and puts your pet under considerable stress. Last, but not least, consider whether or not you have the means to care for an entire litter of pups. Without a reputation in the field, your attempts to sell the pups may be unsuccessful.

feathered. The rump and hind legs down to the hock are covered with thick hair that form the characteristic "trousers." The ruff (mane) and long outer guard hairs and set well apart, giving an intelligent expression. Eye rims are black to dark brown. Eyelashes are white. *Fault:* Unpigmented eye rims. *Disqualification:* Blue eyes.

Ears—Ears conform to head size and blend softly with the wedge-shaped head. The ears are set well apart, and are triangular, slightly rounded at the tips, and held erect. The outer and inner parts of the ear are covered with short, smooth hair, with longer tufts in front of the ear openings. The skin on the inside of the ear is pink or slightly tinged with gray. *Fault:* Flop ears.

Neck: The neck is medium in length, conforming proportionately to the body; strong, carried proudly erect, and blending into the shoulders with a graceful arch.

Forequarters: The shoulders are laid back at an apparent 45-degree angle and are firmly set. The forelegs are parallel and straight, with strong, flexible pasterns to add spring to movement. The elbows are close to the body, turning neither in nor out. Leg length from elbow to ground is approximately equal to half the dog's height at the withers.

Body: The body is strong and compactly built, but not too short-coupled. The length of back from withers to set-on of tail is equal to the height from withers

Correct balance can be a challenging characteristic because of the wide range of allowable sizes. All sizes should be slightly longer than tall. Faults: The top illustration shows an Eskie that is too cobby and high on leg; the Eskie in the lower illustration is too long and low on leg.

to the ground. Females may be slightly longer. The withers are the highest portion of the backline and blend gracefully into the back. The back is straight, level, broad, and muscular. The loins are well muscled and of adequate length to facilitate the easy rhythmic movement and powerful drive of the back legs. The chest is strong, showing broadness and depth. Depth of chest is at

approximate point of elbows. The ribs are well sprung and begin an upsweep behind the ninth rib, which assures adequate room for heart and lung action. The belly has a slight tuck up just behind the ribs.

Hindquarters: The hind legs are muscular and of adequate bone to conform to body size. The upper thighs are well developed and muscled. The stifles lay approximately 30 degrees off the pelvis.

The hock joint is sharply defined and the hocks are well let down. When the dog is standing naturally, the hind legs are parallel when viewed from the rear, turning neither in nor out.

Feet: The feet are compact, oval in shape, and well padded with hair. The pads are tough and deeply cushioned. The feet neither toe in nor out when the dog is standing naturally. Front dewclaws may be removed at the

The breed is divided into three sizes, shown from left to right: Toy, Miniature and Standard. The Toy variety is not recognized by the UKC.

owner's discretion. Rear dewclaws are objectionable and should be removed.

Tail: The tail is set moderately high and is covered with long, profuse hair. It is carried over the back, not necessarily centered, when the dog is alert or moving. When the dog is relaxed, the tail may drop. When hanging down, the tail bone reaches to the hock joint. *Faults:* Tightly curled tail; double hook tail.

Coat: The body is covered with a soft, thick, short undercoat. Longer guard hair grows through the undercoat to form the outer coat. The guard hair is free of any curl or wave. The mane covering the neck area is noticeably thicker, forming the ruff, which is typically more profuse on males than females. The front of the forelegs are covered with short, smooth hair while the back sides are well feathered. The rump and hind legs down to the hock are covered with thick hair that forms the characteristic "trousers." The tail is richly plumed.

Coat length will vary from dog to dog. Quality is more important than quantity.

Color: Pure white is most desired. The *only* other permissible colors are: white with biscuit cream, and cream. *Disqualification:* Any color other than those stated above.

Height: Miniature: Males from 12 inches up to and including 15 inches; Females from 11 inches up to and including 14 inches.

Puppy class only—Minimum permissible heights are 11 inches for males and 10 inches for females.

Standard: Males over 15 inches up to and including 19 inches; Females over 14 inches up to and including 18 inches.

Championship points earned in the Miniature classes are valid in combination with points earned in the Standard classes.

Gait: The American Eskimo is a trotting breed. The dog does not pace at a trotting speed. The stride is quick, agile, and well timed. The gait, viewed from the side, is efficient, balanced, and vigorous, showing good reach in the forequarters matched with a strong rear action drive in the hindquarters during the trot. When walking, the dog will not single track, or brush, but as speed increases, the legs gradually angle inward until the pads fall on a straight line directly under the longitudinal center of the body. When moving, the topline remains strong, level, and firm.

Faults: Any departure from the ideal described in this breed standard is faulted to the extent of the deviation. Structural faults common to all trotting breeds are undesirable in the American Eskimo, even though such faults may not be specifically mentioned herein.

Disqualifications: Unilateral or bilateral cryptorchid. Viciousness or extreme shyness. Blue eyes. Albinism. Blindness. Deafness. Any color other than those stated above. Any alterations of the dog other than allowed by the standard.

SCALE OF POINTS	
General Appearance	15
Movement	15
Head	10
Coat	10
Chest and Ribs	10
Forequarters	10
Hindquarters	10
Back	10
Feet/Legs	5
Tail	5
Total	100

AMERICAN ESKIMO DOG

WHERE TO BEGIN?

If you are convinced that the American Eskimo Dog is the ideal breed for you, it's time to learn about where to find a puppy and what to look for. Locating a litter of American Eskimo pups should not present too much of a problem for the new owner for, although the breed is moderately popular, it does enjoy a dedicated following across the country. You should inquire about breeders who enjoy a good reputation in the breed. You are looking for an established breeder with outstanding dog ethics and a strong commitment to the breed.

New owners should have as many questions as they have doubts. An established breeder is indeed the one to answer your four million questions and make you comfortable with your choice of the American Eskimo. An established breeder will sell you a puppy at a fair price if, and only if, the breeder determines that you are a suitable, worthy owner of his dogs. An established breeder can be relied upon for advice, no matter what time of day or night. A reputable breeder will accept a puppy back, without questions, should you decide that this is not the right dog for you.

When choosing a breeder, reputation is much more important than convenience of location. Do not be overly impressed by breeders who run brag advertisements in the dog presses about their stupendous champions. The real quality breeders are quiet and unassuming. You hear about them

Sound, happy parents produce sound, happy puppies. This youngster and adult radiate the delightful charm that defines the breed's personality.

PUPPY PERSONALITY

When a litter becomes available to you, choosing a pup out of all those adorable faces will not be an easy task! Sound temperament is of utmost importance, but each pup has his own personality and some may be better suited to you than others. A feisty, independent pup will do well in a home with older children and adults, while quiet, shy puppies will thrive in a home with minimal noise and distractions. Your breeder knows the pups best and should be able to guide you in the right direction.

at dog shows and trials, by word of mouth. You may be well advised to avoid the novice who lives only a few miles away. The novice breeder, trying so hard to get rid of that first litter of puppies, is more than accommodating and anxious to sell you one. That breeder may charge you as much as any established breeder. The novice breeder isn't going to interrogate you and your family about your intentions with the puppy, the environment and training you can provide. That breeder will be nowhere to be found when your poorly bred, badly adjusted four-pawed monster starts to growl, spit up at midnight or eat the family cat!

Choosing a breeder is an important first step in dog ownership. Fortunately, the majority of American Eskimo breeders is devoted to the breed and its well-being. New owners should have little problem finding a reputable breeder in their home county or nearby. The AKC and the UKC are able to refer prospective owners to breeders of quality American Eskimos, as can one of the American Eskimo Dog clubs.

Potential owners are encouraged to attend dog shows (or trials) to see the American Eskimos in action, to meet the owners and handlers firsthand and to get an idea of what American Eskimo Dogs look like outside a photographer's lens.

Provided you approach the handlers when they are not busy with the dogs, most will be more than willing to answer questions, recommend breeders and give advice.

Once you have contacted and met a breeder or two and made your choice about which breeder is best suited to your needs, it's time to visit the litter. Litter size varies greatly. Four or five puppies in a Standard litter would be average, with fewer puppies in litters of the Miniature and Toy varieties.

Keep in mind that many top breeders have waiting lists. Sometimes new owners, especially those seeking a show-potential pup, have to wait a year or more for a puppy. If you are really committed to the breeder whom you've selected, then you will wait (and hope for an early

arrival!). If not, you may have to go with your second- or third-choice breeder. Don't be too anxious, however. If the breeder doesn't have a waiting list, or any customers, there is probably a good reason. It's no different than visiting a restaurant with no clientele. The better establishments always have waiting lists—and it's usually worth the wait. Besides, isn't a puppy more important than a meal?

Since you are likely to be choosing an American Eskimo as a pet dog and not a show dog, you simply should select a pup that is friendly, attractive and healthy. You also may have decided if you'd prefer a male or a female Eskie. It can honestly be said that both the male and the female make wonderful companions, but

Potential show dog or purely a pet? It is up to you. Take the breeder's advice as to which pup shows the most promise for the ring and which pup will best fit into your family's home and lifestyle.

HANDLE WITH CARE

You should be extremely careful about handling tiny puppies. Not that you might hurt them, but that the pups' mother may exhibit what is called "maternal aggression." It is a natural, instinctive reaction for the dam to protect her young against anything she interprets as predatory or possibly harmful to her pups. The sweetest, most gentle of bitches, after whelping a litter, often reacts this way, even to her owner.

there are some slight differences to consider. Females may be slightly more independent, and males usually are larger, grander and perhaps just a bit bolder in some cases. Still, there are some very laid-back males and some bitches who are, well, let's just say, properly named! Males also are much more heavily coated. The female is smaller and usually carries less coat. Both males and females shed their coats.

Breeders commonly allow visitors to see their litters by around the fifth or sixth week, and puppies leave for their new homes between the eighth and tenth week, maybe later for a Toy. Breeders who permit their puppies to leave early are more interested in making a profit than in their puppies' well-being. Puppies need to learn the rules of the pack from their dams, and most dams continue teaching the pups manners and dos and don'ts until around the eighth week. Breeders spend significant amounts of time with the American Eskimo toddlers so that the pups are able to interact with the "other species," i.e., humans. Given the long history that dogs and humans have, bonding between the two species is natural but must be nurtured. A well-bred, well-socialized Eskie pup wants nothing more than to be near you and please you.

RECOGNIZING A SOUND AND HEALTHY PUPPY

The American Eskimo puppy that you bring into your home will be your best friend and a member of your family for many years to come. Many well-bred and well-cared-for Eskies live to be 12, 15 or even 17 years of age. Therefore, it is of the utmost importance that the Eskie you select has had every opportunity to begin life in a healthy, stable environment and comes from stock that is both extremely physical and temperamentally sound.

PUPPY APPEARANCE
Your puppy should have a well-fed appearance but not a distended abdomen, which may indicate worms or incorrect feeding, or both. The body should be firm, with a solid feel. The skin of the abdomen should be pale pink and clean, without signs of scratching or rash. Check the hind legs to make certain that dewclaws were removed, if any were present at birth.

The only way you can be assured of this is to go directly to a breeder of American Eskimos who has consistently produced dogs of this kind over the years. A breeder earns this reputation through a well-planned breeding program that has been governed by rigid selectivity. Selective breeding programs are aimed at maintaining the breed's many fine qualities and keeping the breed free of as many genetic weaknesses as possible.

Not all good breeders maintain large kennels. In fact, you are more apt to find that Eskies come from the homes of small hobby breeders who keep only a few dogs and have litters only occasionally. The names of these people are just as likely to appear on the recommended lists from the kennel and breed clubs as the larger kennels that maintain many dogs. Hobby breeders are equally dedicated to breeding quality American Eskimos. A factor in favor of the hobby breeder is their distinct advantage

Puppies use a lot of energy just being puppies, and their rest periods are just as important as periods of activity and exploration.

of being able to raise their puppies in the home environment with all of the accompanying personal attention and socialization.

A healthy Eskie puppy is a bouncy, playful extrovert. Wariness of strangers comes as the puppy begins to mature into adulthood. Never select a puppy that appears shy or listless because you feel sorry for him. Doing so will undoubtedly lead to heartache and expensive veterinary costs. Do not attempt to make up for what the breeder lacked in providing proper care and nutrition. It seldom works.

Ask the breeder if it is possible to take the Eskie puppy to which you are attracted into a different room in the kennel or house in which the pup was raised. The smells will remain the same for the puppy, so he should still feel secure, but doing this will give you an opportunity to

ARE YOU A FIT OWNER?

If the breeder from whom you are buying a puppy asks you a lot of personal questions, do not be insulted. Such a breeder wants to be sure that you will be a fit provider for his puppy.

"YOU BETTER SHOP AROUND!"

Finding a reputable breeder who sells healthy pups is very important, but make sure that the breeder you choose is not only someone you respect but also someone with whom you feel comfortable. Your breeder will be a resource long after you buy your puppy, and you must be able to call with reasonable questions without being made to feel like a pest! If you don't connect on a personal level, investigate some other breeders before making a final decision.

see how the puppy acts away from his littermates. It also will give you an opportunity to inspect the puppy more closely.

Even though American Eskimo puppies are quite small (particularly those of the Toy and Miniature varieties), they should feel sturdy to the touch. Puppies should not feel bony, nor should their abdomens be bloated and extended. A puppy that has just eaten may have a full belly, but the puppy should never appear obese.

A healthy puppy's ears will be pink and clean. Dark discharge or a bad odor could indicate ear mites, a sure sign of lack of cleanliness and poor maintenance. An Eskie puppy's breath should always smell sweet. The pup's teeth must be clean and bright, and there should never be any malformation of the jaw, lips or nostrils. Always check the bite of your selected puppy to be sure that it is neither overshot nor undershot.

The puppy's eyes should be dark and clear—little spots of charcoal on a snow white background. Runny eyes or eyes that appear red and irritated could be caused by myriad problems, none of which indicates a healthy puppy. Coughing and/or diarrhea also are danger signals, as is any discharge from the nose or eruptions on the skin. The fluffy coat should be soft, clean and lustrous.

Sound conformation can be determined even at eight or ten weeks of age. The puppy's legs should be straight, without bumps or malformations. The toes should point straight ahead. The back should be strong and straight, and the little tail will be carried over the pup's back.

The puppy's attitude tells you a great deal about his state of health. Puppies that are feeling "out-of-sorts" react very quickly and will usually find a warm littermate with whom to snuggle up. An under-the-weather pup usually will prefer to stay curled up even when the rest of the "gang" wants to play or go exploring.

There are many "beauty-point" shortcomings that an American Eskimo puppy might have that would in no way inter-

PET INSURANCE

Just like you can insure your car, your house and your own health, you likewise can insure your dog's health. Investigate a pet insurance policy by talking to your vet. Depending on the age of your dog, the breed and the kind of coverage you desire, your policy can be very affordable. Most policies cover accidental injuries, poisoning and thousands of medical problems and illnesses, including cancers. Some carriers also offer routine care and immunization coverage.

fere with his being a wonderful companion, but these faults could be serious drawbacks in the show ring. Many of these things are such that a beginner in the breed might hardly notice. This is why employing the assistance of a good breeder is so important in choosing your pup, whether as solely a pet or as a potential show dog.

All of the foregoing regarding

When you visit a litter, also take the time to look around the breeder's kennel and to meet any adult dogs on the premises. Ensure that all areas are clean and that all dogs are healthy and well-cared-for.

soundness and health in selecting a companion puppy apply to the show puppy as well. In addition to being sound and healthy, the show prospect must also adhere to the standard of the breed very closely.

Like the pet, the show prospect puppy must have a happy, outgoing temperament. He will be a compact little bundle of fluff, never appearing short-legged or out of balance. The show puppy will move around with ease, head held high and tail carried over the back. Dark eyes and black nose, lips and eye rims are required.

COMMITMENT OF OWNERSHIP

After considering all of these factors, you have most likely already made some very important decisions about selecting your puppy. You have chosen the American Eskimo, which means that you have decided which characteristics you want in a dog and what type of dog will best fit into your family and lifestyle. If you have selected a breeder, you have gone a step further—you have done your research and found a responsible, conscientious person who breeds quality American Eskimo Dogs and who should be a reliable source of help as you and your puppy adjust to life together. If you have observed a litter in action, you have obtained a firsthand look at the

YOUR SCHEDULE . . .

If you lead an erratic, unpredictable life, with daily or weekly changes in your work requirements, consider the problems of owning a puppy. The new puppy has to be fed regularly, socialized (loved, petted, handled, introduced to other people) and, most importantly, allowed to go outdoors for housebreaking. As the dog gets older, he can be more tolerant of deviations in his feeding and relief schedule.

ARE YOU PREPARED?

Unfortunately, when a puppy is bought by someone who does not take into consideration the time and attention that dog ownership requires, it is the puppy who suffers when he is either abandoned or placed in a shelter by a frustrated owner. So all of the "homework" you do in preparation for your pup's arrival will benefit you both. The more informed you are, the more you will know what to expect and the better equipped you will be to handle the ups and downs of raising a puppy. Hopefully, everyone in the household is willing to do his part in raising and caring for the pup. The anticipation of owning a dog often brings a lot of promises from excited family members: "I will walk him every day," "I will feed him," "I will housebreak him," etc., but these things take time and effort, and promises can easily be forgotten once the novelty of the new pet has worn off.

dynamics of a puppy "pack" and, thus, you have learned about each pup's individual personality—perhaps you have even found one that particularly appeals to you.

However, even if you have not yet found the American Eskimo puppy of your dreams, observing pups will help you learn to recognize certain behavior and to determine what a pup's behavior indicates about his temperament. You will be able to pick out which pups are the leaders, which ones are less outgoing, which ones are confident, shy, playful, friendly, aggressive, etc. Equally as important, you will learn to recognize what a healthy pup should look and act like. All of these things will help you in your search, and when you find the American Eskimo Dog that was meant for you, you will know it!

Researching your breed,

selecting a responsible breeder and observing as many pups as possible are all important steps on the way to dog ownership. It may seem like a lot of effort…and you have not even taken the pup home yet! Remember, though, you cannot be too careful when it comes to deciding on the type of dog you want and finding out about your prospective pup's background. Buying a puppy is

Of course, a big responsibility of puppy ownership is teaching proper toileting habits. Housebreaking the pup will begin on the very first day that you bring him home.

PEDIGREE VS. REGISTRATION CERTIFICATE

Too often new owners are confused between these two important documents. Your puppy's pedigree, essentially a family tree, is a written record of a dog's genealogy of three generations or more. The pedigree will show you the names as well as performance titles of all dogs in your pup's background. Your breeder must provide you with a registration application, with his part properly filled out. You must complete the application and send it to the AKC with the proper fee. Every puppy must come from a litter that has been AKC-registered by the breeder, born in the USA and from a sire and dam that are also registered with the AKC.

The seller must provide you with complete records to identify the puppy. The AKC requires that the seller provide the buyer with the following: breed; sex, color and markings; date of birth; litter number (when available); names and registration numbers of the parents; breeder's name; and date sold or delivered.

your puppy is not a cuddly stuffed toy or decorative lawn ornament; rather, he is a living creature that will become a real member of your family. You will come to realize that, while buying a puppy is a pleasurable and exciting endeavor, it is not something to be taken lightly. Relax...the fun will start when the pup comes home!

Always keep in mind that a puppy is nothing more than a baby in a furry disguise...a baby who is virtually helpless in a human world and who trusts his owner for fulfillment of his basic needs for survival. In addition to food, water and shelter, your pup needs care, protection, guidance and love. If you are not prepared to commit to this, then you are not prepared to own a dog.

"Wait a minute," you say. "How hard could this be? All of my neighbors own dogs and they seem to be doing just fine. Why should I have to worry about all of this?" Well, you should not worry about it; in fact, you will probably find that once your American Eskimo pup gets used to his new home, he will fall into his place in the family quite naturally. However, it never hurts to emphasize the commitment of dog ownership. With some time and patience, it is really not too difficult to raise a curious and exuberant American Eskimo pup to be a well-adjusted and well-mannered

not—or *should* not be—just another whimsical purchase. This is one instance in which you actually do get to choose your own family! You may be thinking that buying a puppy should be fun—it should not be so serious and so much work. Keep in mind that adult dog—a dog that could be your most loyal friend.

PREPARING PUPPY'S PLACE IN YOUR HOME

Researching your breed and finding a breeder are only two aspects of the "homework" you will have to do before bringing your Eskie puppy home. You will also have to prepare your home and family for the new addition. Much as you would prepare a nursery for a newborn baby, you will need to designate a place in your home that will be the puppy's own. How you prepare your home will depend on how much freedom the dog will be allowed. Whatever you decide, you must ensure that he has a place that he can "call his own."

When you bring your new puppy into your home, you are bringing him into what will become his home as well. Obviously, you did not buy a puppy with the intentions of catering to his every whim and allowing him to "rule the roost," but in order for a puppy to grow into a stable, well-adjusted dog, he has to feel comfortable in his surroundings. Remember, he is leaving the warmth and security of his mother and littermates, as well as the familiarity of the only place he has ever known, so it is important to make his transition as easy as possible. By preparing a place in your home for the puppy,

you are making him feel as welcome as possible in a strange new place. It should not take him long to get used to it, but the sudden shock of being transplanted is somewhat traumatic for a young pup. Imagine how a small child would feel in the same situ-

THE PROBLEM CHILD
Training your puppy takes much patience and can be frustrating at times, but you should see results from your efforts. If you have a puppy that seems untrainable, take him to a trainer or behaviorist. The dog may have a personality problem that requires the help of a professional, or perhaps you need help in learning how to train your dog.

ation—that is how your puppy must be feeling. It is up to you to reassure him and to let him know, "Little Eskie, you are going to like it here!"

TEMPERAMENT COUNTS

Your selection of a good puppy can be determined by your needs. A show potential or a good pet? It is your choice. Every puppy, however, should be of good temperament. Although show-quality puppies are bred and raised with emphasis on physical conformation, responsible breeders strive for equally good temperament. Do not buy from a breeder who concentrates solely on physical beauty at the expense of personality.

WHAT YOU SHOULD BUY

CRATE

To someone unfamiliar with the use of crates in dog training, it may seem like punishment to shut a dog in a crate, but this is not the case at all. More and more breeders and trainers worldwide are recommending crates as preferred tools for pet puppies as well as show puppies.

Crates are not cruel—crates have many humane and highly effective uses in dog care and training. For example, crate training is a popular and very successful housebreaking method. In addition, a crate can keep your dog safe during travel and, perhaps most importantly, a crate provides your dog with a place of his own in your home. It serves as a "doggie bedroom" of sorts—your American Eskimo can curl up in his crate when he wants to sleep or when he just needs a break. Many dogs sleep in their crates overnight. With soft bedding and his favorite toy, a crate becomes a cozy pseudo-den for your dog. Like his ancestors, he too will seek out the comfort and retreat of a den—you just happen to be providing him with something a little more luxurious than what his early ancestors enjoyed.

As far as purchasing a crate, the type that you buy is up to you. It will most likely be one of the two most popular types: wire or fiberglass. There are advantages and disadvantages to each type. For example, a wire crate is more open, allowing the air to flow through and affording the dog a view of what is going on around him. Wire crates are good for use in the home. Fiberglass crates are sturdier and are usually the crates of choice for traveling, although both types can double as travel crates, providing protection for the dog in the car.

The size of the crate is another thing to consider. The variety of your Eskie will deter-mine how large a crate he needs in adulthood, and it is best to get a crate that will accommodate your dog both as a pup and at full size. The recommended crate size for the Standard variety is the intermediate size, #300, approxi-mately 32 inches deep by 22 inches wide by 23 inches high. The Miniature and Toy varieties can best be accommodated in the smaller-sized crates; 21 inches deep by 16 inches wide by 15 inches high should suffice for a Toy, and a Miniature will need one a little larger. Again, the recommended crate sizes will house an adult Eskie of his respective variety, and this is the size that should be purchased when the dog is a puppy.

BEDDING
A soft crate pad and a cuddly blanket in your Eskie's crate will

Your local pet shop will have a variety of crates from which you can select one of a size that will suit your variety of American Eskimo when full grown.

make the crate more comfortable and will help the dog feel at home. First, these things will take the place of the leaves, twigs, etc., that the pup would use in the wild to make a den; the pup can make his own "burrow" in the crate. Although your pup is far removed from his den-making ancestors, the denning instinct is still a part of his genetic makeup. Second, until you take your pup home, he has been sleeping amid the warmth of his mother and littermates, and while a blanket is not the same as a warm, breathing

ing on your expensive shoes and leather sofa. Puppies love to chew; in fact, chewing is a physical need for pups as they are teething, and everything looks appetizing! The full range of your possessions—from old dish rag to Oriental carpet—are fair game in the eyes of a teething pup. Puppies are not all that discerning when it comes to finding something to "sink their teeth into"—everything tastes great!

Eskies are not known for being aggressive chewers. Any standard toys made for dogs should be suitable, but just use common sense in the toys that

Whether trips to the vet, family vacations or weekend journeys to dog shows, you can travel with peace of mind knowing that your Eskie's crate will keep him safe.

body, it still provides heat and something with which to snuggle. You will want to wash your pup's bedding frequently in case he has a potty "accident" in his crate, and replace or remove anything in his crate that becomes ragged and starts to fall apart.

Toys

Toys are a must for dogs of all ages, especially for curious playful pups. Puppies are the "children" of the dog world, and what child does not love toys? Chew toys provide enjoyment for both dog and owner—your dog will enjoy playing with his favorite toys, while you will enjoy the fact that they distract him from chew-

CRATE-TRAINING TIPS

During crate training, you can partition off the section of the crate in which the pup stays. If he is given too big an area, this will hinder your training efforts. Crate training is based on the fact that a dog does not like to soil his sleeping quarters, so it is ineffective to keep a pup in an area that is so big that he can eliminate in one end and get far enough away from it to sleep. Also, you want to make the crate den-like for the pup. Blankets and a favorite toy will make the crate cozy for the small pup; as he grows, you may want to evict some of his "roommates" to make more room. It will take some coaxing at first, but be patient. Given some time to get used to it, your pup will adapt to his new home-within-a-home quite nicely.

you offer. For example, stuffed toys can become de-stuffed in no time. The overly excited pup may ingest the stuffing, which is neither nutritious nor digestible. Similarly, squeaky toys are quite popular, but if a pup "disembowels" one of these, the small plastic squeaker inside can be dangerous if swallowed.

Be careful of natural bones, which have a tendency to splinter into sharp, dangerous pieces. Also be careful of rawhide, which can turn into pieces that are easy to swallow and become a mushy mess on your carpet.

The best thing to do is to supervise your Eskie when he's playing with any potentially destructible toys, and offer him safe sturdy chews, such as nylon bones, for free play. Monitor the condition of all of your pup's toys carefully and get rid of any that have been chewed to the point of becoming potentially dangerous.

LEASH

A nylon leash is probably the best option, as it is the most resistant to puppy teeth should your pup take a liking to chewing on his leash. Of course, this is a habit that should be nipped in the bud, but, if your pup likes to chew on his leash, he has a very slim chance of being able to chew through the strong nylon. Nylon leashes are also lightweight, which is good for a young

American Eskimo who is just getting used to the idea of walking on a leash. For everyday walking and safety purposes, the nylon leash is a good choice.

As your pup grows up and gets used to walking on the leash, you may want to purchase a flexible leash. These leashes allow you to extend the length to give the

TOYS, TOYS, TOYS!

With a big variety of dog toys available, and so many that look like they would be a lot of fun for a dog, be careful in your selection. It is amazing what a set of puppy teeth can do to an innocent-looking toy, so, obviously, safety is a major consideration. Be sure to choose the most durable products that you can find. Hard nylon bones and toys are a safe bet, and many of them are offered in different scents and flavors that will be sure to capture your dog's attention. It is always fun to play a game of fetch with your dog, and there are balls and flying discs that are specially made to withstand dog teeth.

Your Eskie will need a lightweight yet sturdy leash for everyday walks and training.

to wearing the collar, but soon he will not even notice that it is there. Choke collars are made for training, but are not recommended for use on small dogs and coated breeds, so therefore are inappropriate for any variety of American Eskimo.

FOOD AND WATER BOWLS
Your pup will need two bowls, one for food and one for water. You may want two sets of bowls, one for indoors and one for outdoors, depending on where the dog will be fed and where he will be spending time. Stainless steel or sturdy plastic bowls are popular choices. Plastic bowls are more chewable, but dogs tend not to chew on the steel variety, which can be sterilized. It is important to buy sturdy bowls since anything is in danger of being chewed by puppy teeth and you do not want your dog to be constantly chewing apart his bowl (for his safety and for your wallet!).

CLEANING SUPPLIES
Until a pup is housebroken, you will be doing a lot of cleaning. "Accidents" will occur, which is acceptable in the beginning stages of toilet training because the puppy does not know any better. All you can do is be prepared to clean up any accidents as soon as they happen. Old rags and towels, paper towels, newspapers and a safe disinfectant are good to have on hand.

dog a broader area to explore or to shorten the length to keep the dog near you.

COLLAR
Your pup should get used to wearing a collar all the time since you will want to attach his ID tags to it; plus, you have to attach the leash to something! A lightweight nylon collar is a good choice. Make certain that the collar fits snugly enough so that the pup cannot wriggle out of it, but is loose enough so that it will not be uncomfortably tight around the pup's neck. Keep in mind that the Eskie has quite a bit of hair growing around his neck! You should be able to fit a finger between the pup's neck and the collar. It may take some time for your pup to get used

CHOOSE AN APPROPRIATE COLLAR

The **BUCKLE COLLAR** is the standard collar used for everyday purposes. Be sure that you adjust the buckle on growing puppies. Check it every day. It can become too tight overnight! These collars can be made of leather or nylon. Attach your dog's identification tags to this collar.

The **CHOKE COLLAR** is designed for training. It is constructed of highly polished steel so that it slides easily through the stainless steel loop. The idea is that the dog controls the pressure around his neck and he will stop pulling if the collar becomes uncomfortable. It should *not* be used on American Eskimo Dogs of any size, as it is not suitable for small dogs and also will pull and damage the Eskie's heavy coat.

The **HALTER** is for a trained dog that has to be restrained to prevent running away, chasing a cat and the like. Considered the most humane of all collars, it is frequently used on smaller dogs on which collars are not comfortable.

Select durable bowls that are chew-resistant and that can be cleaned easily. You may consider multiple water bowls so that you can keep one in each of the areas where your Eskie spends time.

PHOTO COURTESY OF MIKKI PET PRODUCTS.

BEYOND THE BASICS

The items previously discussed are the bare necessities. You will find out what else you need as you go along—grooming supplies, flea/tick protection, baby gates to partition a room, etc. These things will vary depending on your situation, but it is important that right away you have everything you need to feed and make your American Eskimo Dog comfortable in his first few days at home.

PUPPY-PROOFING YOUR HOME

Aside from making sure that your American Eskimo will be comfortable in your home, you also have to make sure that your home is safe for your American Eskimo. This means taking precautions that your pup will not get into anything he should not get into and that there is nothing within his reach that may harm him should he sniff it, chew it, inspect it, etc. This probably seems obvious since, while you are primarily concerned with your pup's safety, at the same time you do not want your belongings to be ruined. Breakables should be placed out of reach if your dog is to have full run of the house. If he is to be limited to certain places within the house, keep any potentially dangerous items in the "off-limits" areas.

An electrical cord can pose a danger should the puppy decide to taste it—and who is going to convince a pup that it would not make a great chew toy? All cords and wires should be fastened tightly against the wall and kept from puppy teeth. If your Eskie is going to spend time in a crate, make sure that there is nothing near his crate that he can reach if he sticks his curious little nose or paws through the openings. Just as you would with a child, keep all household cleaners and chemicals where the pup cannot reach them.

It is also important to make sure that the outside of your home is safe. Of course, your puppy should never be unsupervised, but a pup let loose in the yard will want to run and explore, and he should be granted that freedom. Do not let a fence give you a false sense of security; you would be surprised at how crafty (and persistent) a dog can be in figuring out how to dig under and squeeze his way through small holes, or to jump or climb over a fence.

The American Eskimo is an excellent jumper. Many Standard Eskies are capable of jumping as high as 4 feet straight in the air from a stand-still position, and Miniatures and Toys are not far behind. Although capable of doing so, they are not normally fence-jumpers or climbers unless neglected and not allowed sufficient human companionship. Nonetheless, the Eskie's jumping

ability should be taken into consideration when enclosing your yard.

The fence must be well embedded into the ground and high enough so that it really is

PLAY'S THE THING

Teaching the puppy to play with his toys in running and fetching games is an ideal way to help the puppy develop muscle, learn motor skills and bond with you, his owner and master. He also needs to learn how to inhibit his bite reflex and never to use his teeth on people, forbidden objects and other animals in play. Whenever you play with your puppy, you make the rules. This becomes an important message to your puppy in teaching him that you are the pack leader and control everything he does in life. Once your dog accepts you as his leader, your relationship with him will be cemented for life.

NATURAL TOXINS

Examine your grass and landscaping before bringing your puppy home. Many varieties of plants have leaves, stems or flowers that are toxic if ingested, and you can depend on a curious puppy to investigate them.

If you see your dog carrying a piece of vegetation in his mouth, approach him in a quiet, disinterested manner, avoid eye contact, pet him and gradually remove the plant from his mouth. Alternatively, offer him a treat and maybe he'll drop the plant on his own accord. Be sure no toxic plants are growing in your own yard or kept in your home. Ask your vet for information on poisonous plants or research them at your library.

impossible for your dog to get over it; a height of at least 5 feet should suffice. Be sure to secure any gaps in the fence, and check the fence periodically to ensure that it is in good shape and make repairs as needed. A very determined (or bored) pup may return to the same spot to "work on it" until he is able to get through.

FIRST TRIP TO THE VET

You have selected your puppy, and your home and family are ready. Now all you have to do is collect your American Eskimo from the breeder and the fun begins, right? Well…not so fast. Something else you need to plan is your pup's first trip to the veterinarian. Perhaps your breeder can recommend someone in the area who specializes in American Eskimo Dogs or other spitz-type breeds, or maybe you know some other American Eskimo owners who can suggest a good vet. Either way, you should have an appointment arranged for your pup before you pick him up.

The pup's first visit will consist of an overall examination to make sure that the pup does not have any problems that are not apparent to you. The vet will also set up a schedule for the pup's vaccinations; the breeder will inform you of which ones the pup has already received and the vet can continue from there.

INTRODUCTION TO THE FAMILY

Everyone in the house will be excited about the puppy's coming home and will want to pet him and play with him, but it is best to make the introduction low-key so as not to overwhelm the puppy. He is apprehensive already. It is the first time he has been separated from his mother and the breeder, and the ride to your home is likely to be the first time he has been in a car. The last thing you want to do is smother him, as this will only frighten him further. This is not to say that human contact is not extremely necessary at this stage, because this is the time when a connection between the pup and his human family is formed. Gentle petting and soothing words should help console him, as well as just putting him down and letting him explore on his own (under your watchful eye, of course).

CHEMICAL TOXINS

Scour your garage for potential puppy dangers. Remove weed killers, pesticides and antifreeze materials. Antifreeze is highly toxic and just a few drops can kill a puppy or an adult dog. The sweet taste attracts the animal, who will quickly consume it from the floor or pavement.

The pup may approach the family members or may busy himself with exploring for a while. Gradually, each person should spend some time with the pup, one at a time, crouching down to get as close to the pup's level as possible, letting him sniff each person's hands and petting him gently. He definitely needs human attention and he needs to be touched—this is how to form an immediate bond. Just remember that the pup is experiencing many things

A fenced-in yard is a wonderful place for your Eskie to run and explore, but ensure that the fence is escape-proof and that nothing growing in the yard is harmful to dogs.

for the first time, at the same time. There are new people, new noises, new smells and new things to investigate, so be gentle, be affectionate and be as comforting as you can be.

PUP'S FIRST NIGHT HOME

You have traveled home with your new charge safely in his crate. He's been to the vet for a thorough check-up; he's been weighed, his papers have been examined and perhaps he's even been vaccinated and wormed as well. He's met (and licked!) the whole family, including the excited children and the less-than-happy cat. He's explored his area, his new bed, the yard and anywhere else he's been permitted. He's eaten his first meal at home and relieved himself in the proper place. He's heard lots of new sounds, smelled new friends and seen more of the outside world than ever before...and that was just the first day! He's worn out and is ready for bed...or so you think!

It's puppy's first night home and you are ready to say "Good night." Keep in mind that this is his first night ever to be sleeping alone. His dam and littermates are no longer at paw's length and he's a bit scared, cold and lonely. Be reassuring to your new family member, but this is not the time to spoil him and give in to his inevitable whining.

Puppies whine. They whine to let others know where they are and hopefully to get company out of it. Place your pup in his new bed or crate in his designated area and close the crate door. Mercifully, he may fall asleep without a peep. When the inevitable occurs, however, ignore the whining—he is fine.

FEEDING TIPS

You will probably start feeding your pup the same food that he has been getting from the breeder; the breeder should give you a few days' supply to start you off. Although you should not give your pup too many treats, you will want to have puppy treats on hand for coaxing, training, rewards, etc. Be careful, though, as a small pup's calorie requirements are relatively low and a few treats can add up to almost a full day's worth of calories without the required nutrition.

Be strong and keep his interest in mind. Do not allow yourself to feel guilty and visit the pup. He will fall asleep eventually.

Many breeders recommend placing a piece of bedding from the pup's former home in his new bed so that he recognizes and is comforted by the scent of his littermates. Others still advise placing a hot-water bottle in the bed for warmth. The latter may be a good idea provided the pup doesn't attempt to suckle—he'll get good and wet, and may not fall asleep so fast.

Puppy's first night can be somewhat stressful for both the pup and his new family. Remember that you are setting the tone of nighttime at your house. Unless you want to play with your pup every night at 10 p.m., midnight and 2 a.m., don't initiate the habit. Your family will thank you, and eventually so will your pup!

A wire pen, also called an "ex-pen," can be transported easily to provide your Eskie with an area of safe confinement in which he can play wherever you go.

IN DUE TIME

It will take at least two weeks for your puppy to become accustomed to his new surroundings. Give him lots of love, attention, handling, frequent opportunities to relieve himself, a diet he likes to eat and a place he can call his own.

PREVENTING PUPPY PROBLEMS

SOCIALIZATION

Now that you have done all of the preparatory work and have helped your pup get accustomed to his new home and family, it is about time for you to have some fun! Socializing your Eskie pup gives you the opportunity to show off your new friend, and your pup gets to reap the benefits of being

PUP MEETS WORLD

Thorough socialization includes not only meeting new people but also being introduced to new experiences such as riding in the car, having his coat brushed, hearing the television, walking in a crowd—the list is endless. The more your pup experiences, and the more positive the experiences are, the less of a shock and the less frightening it will be for your pup to encounter new things as he grows up.

exposed to other people, animals and situations. This will help him become well adjusted as he grows up and less prone to being timid or fearful of the new things he will encounter. Of course, he must not come into close contact with dogs you don't know well until his course of injections is fully complete.

Your pup's socialization began with the breeder, but now it is your responsibility to continue it. The socialization he receives until the age of 12 weeks is the most critical, as this is the time when he forms his impressions of the outside world. Be especially careful during the eight-to-ten-week-old period, also known as the fear period. The interaction he receives during this time should be gentle and reassuring. Lack of socialization, and/or negative experiences during the socialization period, can manifest itself in fear and aggression as the dog grows up; shyness and over-wariness of strangers also can be problems in an Eskie that has not been properly socialized. Your puppy needs lots of positive interaction, which of course includes human contact, affection, handling and exposure to other animals.

Once your pup has received his necessary vaccinations, feel free to take him out and about (on his leash, of course). Walk him around the neighborhood, take him on your daily errands, let

an adorable furry snowball that people will want to pet and, in general, think is absolutely precious!

Besides getting to know his new family, your puppy should be people pet him, let him meet other dogs and pets, etc. Puppies do not have to try to make friends; there will be no shortage of people who will want to introduce themselves. Just make sure that you carefully supervise each meeting. If the neighborhood children want to say hello, for example, that is great—children and pups most often make great companions. However, sometimes an excited child can unintentionally handle a pup too roughly, or an overzealous pup can playfully nip a little too hard. You want to make socialization experiences positive ones. What a pup learns during this very formative stage will affect his attitude toward future encounters. You want your dog to be comfortable around everyone. A pup that has a bad experience with a child may grow up to be a dog that is shy around or aggressive toward children.

CONSISTENCY IN TRAINING

Dogs, being pack animals, naturally need a leader, or else they try to establish dominance in their packs. When you welcome a dog into your family, the choice of who becomes the leader and who becomes the "pack" is entirely up to you! Your pup's intuitive quest for dominance, coupled with the fact that it is nearly impossible to look at an adorable American Eskimo pup, with his sparkling dark eyes, and not cave in, give

MANNERS MATTER
During the socialization process, a puppy should meet people, experience different environments and definitely be exposed to other canines. Through playing and interacting with other dogs, your puppy will learn lessons, ranging from controlling the pressure of his jaws by biting his littermates to the inner-workings of the canine pack that he will apply to his human relationships for the rest of his life. That is why removing a puppy from the litter too early (before eight weeks) can be detrimental to the pup's development.

the pup almost an unfair advantage in getting the upper hand! A pup will definitely test the waters to see what he can and cannot do. Do not give in to those pleading eyes—stand your ground when it comes to disciplining the pup and make sure that all family members do the same. It will only confuse the pup if Mother tells him to get off the sofa when he is used to sitting up there with Father to watch the nightly news. Avoid discrepancies by having all members of the household decide on the rules before the pup even comes home…and be consistent in enforcing them! Early training shapes the dog's personality, so you cannot be unclear in what you expect.

COMMON PUPPY PROBLEMS

The best way to prevent puppy problems is to be proactive in stopping an undesirable behavior as soon as it starts. The old saying "You can't teach an old dog new tricks" does not necessarily hold true, but it *is* true that it is much easier to discourage bad behavior in a young developing pup than to wait until the pup's bad behavior becomes the adult dog's bad habit. There are some problems that are especially prevalent in puppies as they develop.

Chew toys keep your Eskie's teeth and mind occupied, and many toys are designed to provide interaction between dog and owner.

NIPPING

As puppies start to teethe, they feel the need to sink their teeth into anything available…unfortunately, that usually includes your fingers, arms, hair and toes. You may find this behavior cute for the first five seconds…until you feel just how sharp those puppy teeth are. Nipping is something you want to discourage immediately and consistently with a firm "No!" (or whatever number of firm "Nos" it takes for him to understand that you mean business). Then, replace your finger with an appropriate chew toy. While this behavior is merely annoying when the dog is young, it can become dangerous as your American Eskimo's adult teeth grow in and his jaws develop, and he continues to think it is okay to gnaw on human appendages. Your American Eskimo does not mean any harm with a friendly nip, but he also does not know that a friendly nip does not feel so friendly to you!

CRYING/WHINING

Your pup will often cry, whine, whimper, howl or make some type of commotion when he is left alone. This is basically his way of calling out for attention to make sure that you know he is there and that you have not forgotten about him. Your puppy feels insecure when he is left alone, when you are out of the

CHEWING TIPS

Chewing goes hand in hand with nipping in the sense that a teething puppy is always looking for a way to soothe his aching gums. In this case, instead of chewing on you, he may have taken a liking to your favorite shoe or something else that he should not be chewing. Again, realize that this is a normal canine behavior that does not need to be discouraged, only redirected. Your pup just needs to be taught what is acceptable to chew on and what is off-limits. Consistently tell him "No!" when you catch him chewing on something forbidden and give him a chew toy.

Conversely, praise him when you catch him chewing on something appropriate. In this way, you are discouraging the inappropriate behavior and reinforcing the desired behavior. The puppy's chewing should stop after his adult teeth have come in, but an adult dog continues to chew for various reasons—perhaps because he is bored, needs to relieve tension or just likes to chew. That is why it is important to redirect his chewing when he is still young.

house and he is in his crate or when you are in another part of the house and he cannot see you. The noise he is making is an expression of the anxiety he feels at being alone, so he needs to be taught that being alone is okay. You are not actually training the dog to stop making noise; rather, you are training him to feel comfortable when he is alone and thus removing the need for him to make the noise.

This is where the crate with cozy bedding and a toy comes in handy. You want to know that your pup is safe when you are not there to supervise, and you know that he will be safe in his crate rather than roaming freely about the house. In order for the pup to stay in his crate without making a fuss, he first needs to be comfort-able in his crate. On that note, it is extremely important that the crate is never used as a form of punishment; this will cause the pup to view the crate as a negative place, rather than as a place of his own for safety and retreat.

Accustom the pup to the crate in short, gradually increasing time intervals in which you put him in the crate, maybe with a treat, and stay in the room with him. If he cries or makes a fuss, do not go to him, but stay in his sight. Gradually he will realize that staying in his crate is just fine without your help, and it will not be so traumatic for him when you are not around. You may want to leave the radio on softly when you leave the house; the sound of human voices may be comforting to him.

FEEDING CONSIDERATIONS

Every breeder of every dog, regardless of breed, has his own particular way of feeding. Most breeders give the new owner a written record that details the amount and kind of food that the puppy has been receiving, along with recommendations about how to continue feeding as the puppy grows up. Do follow these recommendations to the letter at least for the first month or two after the puppy comes to live with you. Following the prescribed procedure will reduce the chance of upset stomach and loose stools.

Along with indicating the type and amount of food, the diet sheet should indicate the number of times per day that your puppy has been accustomed to being fed and the kind of vitamin supplementation, if any, that he has been receiving. Usually a breeder's diet sheet projects the increases and changes in food that will be necessary as your puppy grows from week to week. If the sheet does not include this information, ask the breeder for suggestions regarding increases and eventual changes to the puppy's diet.

If you do your best not to change the puppy's diet when you first bring him home, you will be less apt to run into digestive problems and diarrhea. Diarrhea is very serious in young puppies.

STORING DOG FOOD

You must store your dry dog food carefully. Open packages of dog food quickly lose their vitamin value, usually within 90 days of being opened. Mold spores and vermin could also contaminate the food.

Puppies with diarrhea can dehydrate very rapidly, causing severe problems and even death.

If it is necessary to change your Eskie puppy's diet for any reason, it should be done gradually, over a period of a few days. Begin by mixing a spoonful or two of the new food in with the old food, gradually increasing the ratio of new food to old food until the meal consists entirely of the new product.

In order for a canine diet to qualify as "complete and balanced" in the United States, it must meet standards set by the Subcommittee on Canine Nutrition of the National Research Council of the National Academy of Sciences. Most commercial foods manufactured for dogs meet these standards and prove this by listing the ingredients contained in the food on every package or can. The ingredients are listed in descending order, with the main ingredient listed first.

Through centuries of domestication, we have made our dogs entirely dependent upon us for their well-being. Therefore, we are entirely responsible for duplicating the food balance that the wild dog finds in Nature. The domesticated dog's diet must include protein, carbohydrates, fats, roughage and small amounts of essential minerals and vitamins. Finding commercially prepared diets that contain all of the neces-

FOOD PREFERENCE
Selecting the best dog food is difficult. There is no majority consensus among veterinary scientists as to the value of nutrient analysis (protein, fat, fiber, moisture, ash, cholesterol, minerals, etc.). All agree that feeding trials are what matter most, but you also have to consider the individual dog. The dog's weight, age and activity level, and what pleases his taste, all must be considered. It is best to take the advice of your veterinarian. Every dog's dietary requirements vary, even during the lifetime of a particular dog.

If your dog is fed a good dry food, he does not require supplements of meat or vegetables. Dogs do appreciate a little variety in their diets, so you may choose to stay with the same brand but vary the flavor. Alternatively, you may wish to add a little flavored stock to give a difference to the taste.

TIPPING THE SCALES

Good nutrition is vital to your dog's health, but many people end up over-feeding or giving unnecessary supple-ments. Here are some common doggie diet don'ts:

• Adding things like yogurt and cheese to your dog's diet may seem like a good idea for coat and skin care, but dairy products can be very fattening and can cause indigestion.

• Diets high in fat will not cause heart attacks in dogs but will certainly cause your dog to gain weight.

• Most importantly, don't assume your dog will simply stop eating once he doesn't need any more food. Given the chance, he will eat you out of house and home!

sary nutrients will not present a problem. A visit to your local pet store will reveal how vast an array from which you will be able to select. Among the many varieties of dog food are canned, dry, semi-moist, "scientifically fortified," "all-natural" and the list goes on. Fresh water and a properly prepared, balanced diet that contains the essential nutrients in correct proportions are all that a healthy American Eskimo needs to be offered.

It is important to remember that all dogs, whether they are American Eskimo Dogs, Chihuahuas, Great Danes or anything in between, are carnivo-rous (meat-eating) animals. While the vegetable content of your Eskie's diet should not be over-looked, a dog's physiology and anatomy are based upon carnivo-rous food acquisition. Protein and fat are absolutely essential to the well-being of your dog. In fact, it is wise to add a teaspoon or two of vegetable oil or bacon drip-pings to your dog's diet, particu-larly during the winter months in colder climates.

It is also important to under-stand that commercially prepared dog foods do contain all of the nutrients that your Eskie needs. It is therefore unnecessary to add vitamin supplements to these diets except in special circum-stances prescribed by your veteri-narian. Over-supplementation and forced growth are now looked upon by some breeders as major contributors to many skeletal abnormalities found in the pure-bred dogs of the day.

A great deal of controversy exists today regarding orthopedic problems such as hip dysplasia and patellar (knee) luxation that can afflict all breeds. Some claim that these problems are entirely hereditary conditions, but many others feel that these problems can be exacerbated by overuse of mineral and vitamin supplements for puppies.

In giving vitamin supplemen-tation, one should never exceed

"DOES THIS COLLAR MAKE ME LOOK FAT?"

While humans may obsess about how they look and how trim their bodies are, many people believe that extra weight on their dogs is a good thing. The truth is, pets should not be over- or under-weight, as both can lead to or signal sickness. In order to tell how fit your pet is, run your hands over his ribs. Are his ribs buried under a layer of fat or are they sticking out considerably? If your pet is within his normal weight range, you should be able to feel the ribs easily, but they should not protrude abnormally. If you stand above him, the outline of his body should resemble an hourglass. Some breeds do tend to be leaner while some are a bit stockier, but making sure your dog is the right weight for his breed will certainly contribute to his good health.

the amount prescribed by the vet. Many Eskie breeders insist that all recommended dosages be halved before including them in a dog's diet. Still other breeders feel that no supplementation should be given at all, believing that a balanced diet, which includes animal protein, an appropriate amount of milk products, some fat and a small amount of bone meal to provide calcium, is all that is necessary and beneficial.

Pregnant and lactating bitches may require supplementation of

some kind, but here again it is not a case of "if a little is good, a lot would be a great deal better." Extreme caution is advised in this case and of course must be discussed with your veterinarian.

There are now any number of commercially prepared diets for dogs with special dietary needs. The overweight, underweight or geriatric dog can have his nutritional needs met, as can puppies and growing dogs. The calorie content of each of these foods is adjusted accordingly. With the correct amount of the right foods and the proper amount of exercise, your Eskie should stay in top shape. Again, common sense must prevail. Too many calories will increase weight and cutting back on calories will reduce weight.

Fed with any regularity at all, refined sugars can cause your Eskie to become obese and will definitely create tooth decay.

With heavily coated dogs, it's sometimes hard to determine if they are of correct weight. To avoid your Eskie's becoming overweight and to reinforce polite behavior, never indulge him with "people foods" and never give in to his begging at the table.

Candy does not exist in the wild and canine teeth are not genetically disposed to handling sugars. Do not feed your Eskie sweets, and avoid products that contain sugar to any high degree. Chocolate, besides being high in sugar, is toxic to dogs and can cause death even in small amounts.

Occasionally, a young Eskie going through the teething period or a female coming into season will go "off" his or her food. The concerned owner's first response often is to tempt the dog by hand-feeding special treats and foods that the problem eater seems to prefer. This practice only serves to compound the problem. Once a dog learns to play the waiting game, he will turn up his nose at anything other than his favorite food, knowing full well that what he wants to eat will eventually arrive.

Because your American Eskimo's food has a bearing on coat, health and temperament, it is essential that the most suitable diet is selected for an Eskie of his age. It is fair to say, however, that even experienced owners can be perplexed by the enormous range of foods available. Only understanding what is best for your dog will help you reach an informed decision. When selecting your dog's diet, three stages of development must be considered: the puppy stage, the adult stage and the senior stage.

PUPPY STAGE

Puppies instinctively want to suck milk from their mother's teats; a normal puppy will exhibit this behavior just a few moments following birth. If puppies do not attempt to suckle within the first half-hour or so, they should be encouraged to do so by placing them on the nipples, having selected ones with plenty of milk. This early milk supply is important in providing the essential colostrum, which protects the puppies during the first eight to ten weeks of their lives. Although a mother's milk is much better than any commercially prepared milk formula, despite there being some excellent ones available, if the puppies do not feed, the breeder will have to feed them by

CHANGE IN DIET

As your dog's caretaker, you know the importance of keeping his diet consistent, but sometimes when you run out of food or if you're on vacation, you have to make a change quickly. Some dogs will experience digestive problems, but most will not. If you are planning on changing your dog's menu, do so gradually to ensure that your dog will not have any problems. Over a period of four to five days, slowly add some new food to your dog's old food, increasing the percentage of new food each day.

hand. For those with less experience, advice from a veterinarian is important so that not only the right quantity of milk is fed but also that of correct quality, fed at suitably frequent intervals, usually every two hours during the first few days of life.

Puppies should be allowed to nurse from their mother for about the first six weeks, although, starting around the third or fourth week, the breeder will begin to introduce small portions of suitable solid food. Most breeders like

Situations arise when puppies need to be bottle-fed in the early weeks of life. Special formulas are made to simulate the mother's milk as closely as possible.

FEEDING TIPS

- Dog food must be served at room temperature, neither too hot nor too cold. Fresh water, changed often and served in a clean bowl, is mandatory, especially when feeding dry food.
- Never feed your dog from the table while you are eating, and never feed your dog leftovers from your own meal. They usually contain too much fat and too much seasoning.
- Dogs must chew their food. Hard pellets are excellent; soups and stews are to be avoided.
- Don't add leftovers or any extras to commercial dog food. The normal food is usually balanced, and adding something extra destroys the balance.
- Except for age-related changes, dogs do not require dietary variations. They can be fed the same diet, day after day, without becoming bored or ill.

to introduce alternate milk and meat meals initially, building up to weaning time.

By the time the puppies are seven or a maximum of eight weeks old, they should be fully weaned and fed solely on a proprietary puppy food. Selection of the most suitable, good-quality diet at this time is essential, for a puppy's fastest growth rate is during the first year of life. Your vet and breeder should be able to offer good advice in this regard. The frequency of meals will be reduced over time, and the transition from growth-formula food to an adult-maintenance diet can

DO DOGS HAVE TASTE BUDS?
Watching a dog "wolf" or gobble his food, seemingly without chewing, leads an owner to wonder whether his dog can taste anything. Yes, dogs have taste buds, with sensory perception of sweet, salty and sour. Puppies are born with fully mature taste buds.

begin after the pup reaches ten months of age.

Again, puppy and junior diets should be well balanced for the needs of your dog so that, except in certain circumstances, additional vitamins, minerals and proteins will not be required and can indeed prove harmful.

ADULT DIETS

A dog is considered an adult when he has stopped growing. In the Eskie, full size comes early, at about 9 or 10 months of age, while full maturity comes later—for females at about 18 months and for dogs at about 24 months. Using full size as a guide, in general the diet of an American Eskimo can be changed to an adult one after 10 months of age. Depending upon the individual dog and his general condition (weight, activity level, etc.), the maintenance diet can be used with most Eskies until around 10 years of age or even older.

Again you should rely upon your vet and breeder to recommend an acceptable maintenance diet. Major dog-food manufacturers specialize in this type of food, and it is merely necessary for you to select the one best suited to your dog's needs. For example, active dogs will have different requirements than dogs who live more sedate lives.

SENIOR DIETS

As dogs get older, their metabolism changes. The older dog usually exercises less, moves more slowly and sleeps more. This change in lifestyle and physiological performance requires a change in diet. Since these changes take place slowly, they might not be recognizable. What is easily recognizable is weight gain. By continuing to feed your dog an adult-maintenance diet when he is slowing down metabolically, your dog will gain weight. Obesity in an older dog compounds the health problems that already accompany old age.

As your dog gets older, few of his organs function up to par. The kidneys slow down and the intestines become less efficient. These age-related factors are best handled with a change in diet and a change in feeding schedule to give smaller portions that are more easily digested. Ten years might be the average age at which to consider an Eskie as a "senior" and to consult your vet about changing your Eskie's diet. There is no single best diet for every older dog. While many dogs do well on light or senior diets, other dogs do better on other special premium diets such as lamb and rice. Be sensitive to your senior Eskie's diet, as this will help control other problems that may arise with your old friend.

WATER

Just as your dog needs proper nutrition from his food, water is an essential "nutrient" as well. Water keeps the dog's body properly hydrated and promotes normal function of the body's systems. During the housebreaking process, it is necessary to keep an eye on how much water your American Eskimo Dog is drinking, but, once he is reliably trained, he should have access to clean fresh water at all times, especially if you feed dry food. Make certain that the dog's water bowl is clean, and change the water often.

EXERCISE

All dogs require some form of exercise, regardless of breed. A sedentary lifestyle is as harmful to a dog as it is to a person. The American Eskimo Dog is a fairly active breed that enjoys exercise, but you don't have to be an Olympic athlete to provide your dog with a sufficient amount of activity! Exercising your American Eskimo can be enjoyable and healthy for both of you.

DRINK, DRANK, DRUNK— MAKE IT A DOUBLE

In both humans and dogs, as well as other living organisms, water forms the major part of nearly every body tissue. Naturally, we take water for granted, but without it, life as we know it would cease.

For dogs, water is needed to keep their bodies functioning biochemically. Additionally, water is needed to replace the water lost while panting. Unlike humans, who are able to sweat to dissipate heat, dogs must pant to cool down, thereby losing the vital water that their bodies need to regulate their body temperatures. Humans lose electrolyte-containing products and other body-fluid components through sweating; dogs do not lose anything except water.

Water is essential always, but especially so when the weather is hot or humid or when your dog is exercising or working vigorously.

Walks with you, a swim, games in the yard...the Eskie will enjoy them all!

Walks with you, a swim, games in the yard...the Eskie will enjoy them all!

Within reason, most anything you can do, your Eskie can do, too. Long morning walks, hikes over mountain trails, exploring tide pools along the beach—your Eskie will enjoy and benefit from these activities as much as you will. On the other hand, if your own exercise proclivities lie closer to a walk around the block than to a ten-mile marathon, your Eskie can be just as satisfied. The American Eskimo is not a breed that requires taking your energy level to its outer limits. Most Eskies are very "busy" dogs; in fact, if your Eskie shares his life with young children or other dogs, he could easily be getting all of the exercise he needs to stay fit. The Eskie is always ready for a romp or to invent some new game that entails plenty of aerobic activity.

Slow steady exercise that keeps your canine companion's

heart rate in the working area will do nothing but extend his life. If your Eskie is getting his exercise with you at his side, you are increasing the chances that the two of you will enjoy each other's company for many more years to come.

Naturally, common sense must be used regarding the extent and intensity of the exercise you give your American Eskimo. Remember, young puppies have short bursts of energy and then require long rest periods. No puppy of any breed should be forced to accompany you on extended runs or to overdo it in any way. Serious injuries can result. Again—short exercise periods and long rest stops for any Eskie under 10–12 months of age.

Most adult Eskies will willingly walk as far as, or perhaps further than, their owners are inclined to go. Daily walks combined with some ball-retrieving or game-playing in the yard can keep the average Eskie in fine fettle.

Caution and common sense must be exercised in hot weather, of course. Plan your walks for the first thing in the morning if at all possible. If you can not arrange to do this, wait until the sun has set and the outdoor temperature has dropped to a comfortable degree.

Cold weather, even temperatures hovering around the zero-degree mark, are no problem at all for the American Eskimo. The only warm clothing required for your winter walks will be yours—as long as the two of you keep moving! Do not, however, allow your Eskie to remain wet if the two of you get caught in the rain or snow. At the very least, you should towel-dry the wet Eskie. Better still, use a blow dryer on the lowest setting to make sure that your Eskie is thoroughly dry and mat-free after outdoor exercise in wet weather.

GROOMING

Proper brushing is all the grooming that your Eskie will ever need unless he is going to a dog show. If the latter is the case, there are a few "tricks of the trade" that the breeder from whom you purchased your Eskie can teach you that will make your little fellow look picture-pretty.

The breeder from whom you purchased your Eskie puppy will have begun to accustom the puppy to grooming just as soon as there was enough hair to brush. You must continue on with grooming sessions or begin them at once if for some reason they have not been started. You and your Eskie will spend many hours involved with this activity over a lifetime, so it is imperative for you both to learn to cooperate in the endeavor to make it an easy and pleasant experience.

You will need to invest in a grooming table with a non-slip surface, two brushes (a wire slicker brush, also called a "rake," and a pin brush, sometimes called a "Poodle brush"), a steel comb, barber's scissors and a pair of nail clippers. For the finish work, you will need a commercial coat conditioner and a spray bottle. Consider the fact that you will be using this equipment for many years, so buy the best of these items that you can afford.

Start by having the pup secure on the grooming table. Make sure that the table on which you groom is of a height at which you can work comfortably either sitting or standing. Do not attempt to groom your Eskie puppy on the floor,

DEADLY DECAY
Did you know that periodontal disease (a condition of the bone and gums surrounding a tooth) can be fatal? Making toothbrushing a regular part of your grooming routine and having your dog's teeth and mouth checked yearly can prevent it.

Your local pet shop should have all of the grooming tools necessary to properly care for your Eskie's coat and keep him looking in top condition.

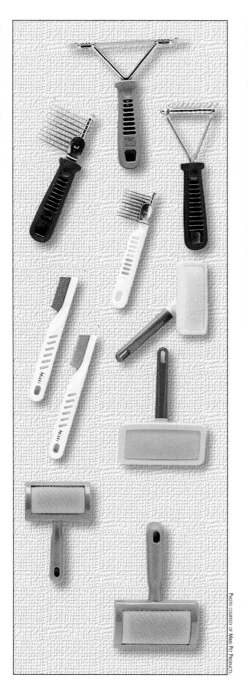

PHOTO COURTESY OF MIKKI PET PRODUCTS.

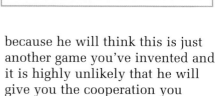

GROOMING EQUIPMENT

How much grooming equipment you purchase will depend on how much grooming you are going to do. Here are some basics:

- Slicker brush
- Pin brush
- Metal comb
- Scissors
- Rubber mat
- Dog shampoo
- Spray hose attachment
- Blow dryer
- Towels
- Ear cleaner
- Cotton balls
- Nail clippers
- Dental-care products

because he will think this is just another game you've invented and it is highly unlikely that he will give you the cooperation you need.

The Eskie puppy should be taught to lie on his side to be groomed. He will be kept in that position for most of the grooming process. The puppy will also have to assume the sitting and standing positions during grooming, but he will be lying down for most of it, and this position is more difficult for the puppy to learn. The Eskie trained to lie quietly on his side will prove to be a true godsend when the dog is fully grown and has developed a mature coat.

Begin training the puppy to lie on his side by picking the puppy up as you would a lamb, with his side against your chest and your arms wrapped around the puppy's body. Lay the puppy down on the grooming table and release your arms, but keep your chest pressed lightly down on the puppy's side. Speak reassuringly to the puppy, stroking his head and rump. (This is a good time to practice the stay command.) Do this a number of times before you attempt to do any grooming. Repeat the process until your puppy understands what he is supposed to do when you place him on the grooming table.

Start brushing your Eskie for a few minutes each day while he is still a puppy to get him accustomed to the grooming routine.

Start with the slicker brush and begin what is called "line brushing" at the top of the shoulder at the base of the neck. Part the hair in a straight line from the front of the shoulder straight on down to the bottom of the chest. Brush through the hair to the right and left of the part, lightly spraying the area with the coat conditioner as you go. Start at the skin and brush out to the very end of the hair. Do a small section at a time and continue on down the part. When you reach the bottom of the part, return to the top and make another part just to the right of the first line you brushed. Part, brush and spray. You will repeat this process, working toward the rear until you reach the puppy's tail.

The ruff around the Eskie's neck can be brushed outward to accentuate its fullness.

Be especially careful to attend to the hard-to-reach areas under the upper legs where they join the body. Mats occur in these areas very rapidly, especially during the time when the Eskie is shedding the puppy coat. Should you encounter a mat that does not brush out easily use your fingers

The backs of the rear pasterns can be trimmed for neatness; besides the feet, this is the only trimming allowed for the show ring.

and the steel comb to separate the hairs as much as possible. Do not cut or pull out the matted hair. Apply baby powder or one of the especially prepared grooming powders directly to the mat and brush it completely from the skin outward.

When you have finished one side, turn the puppy over and complete the entire process on the other side—part, spray, brush. As your Eskie becomes accustomed to this process, you may find that the puppy considers grooming time to be naptime! You may have to lift your puppy into sitting position to arouse him from his slumber.

While the puppy is sitting, you can groom the hair of the chest and neck. Be particularly thorough in the area right behind the ears, as it is highly mat-prone. Use the line-brushing method here as well. Next, stand the puppy up and groom the tail. Check the longer hair of the "pants" on the rear legs to make sure they are thoroughly brushed, especially around the area of the anus and genitalia. Needless to say, it is important to be extremely careful when brushing in these areas, as they are extremely sensitive and easily injured.

Use your barber's scissors to trim the long or shaggy hairs around your Eskie's feet. If your Eskie is not a show dog, you may trim his whiskers off if you wish; this is optional, however. Many Eskie owners prefer to leave the whiskers on, and no trimming of the whiskers is allowed for the show ring.

Brush the hair around the head, shoulders and the back toward the front of the dog. Do the same with the hair of the tail. Brush the chest hair downward and do the same with the hair on the sides of the dog. Your puppy is now groomed and looking just as sweet as he acts!

Grooming the adult coat is a bit different. Not only is the Eskie's adult hair of an entirely different texture, it is much longer and much thicker. By this time, you will have realized that the pin brush, with its longer bristles set in rubber, is better for line-brushing the adult Eskie than the slicker brush that you used through puppyhood. The method of brushing the adult coat is the same as that used on the puppy. The obvious difference is that you have more dog and more hair.

The adult Eskie's hair is actually much easier to cope with than the puppy coat. The ease of working with the Eskie's adult coat, plus your own experience in the grooming routine, combine to make the task far easier than what one might expect. Ten industriously applied minutes each day with a brush, plus a thorough weekly session, will keep your Eskie looking in the best of shape.

On the other hand, if the coat is neglected and becomes matted,

The Eskie's full white coat is his crowning glory. Attention to grooming will keep the coat mat-free, healthy and looking beautiful.

you will indeed have a difficult time ahead of you. The coat can become "felted" with mats and you may have to resort to having a veterinarian or groomer shave the matted-to-the-skin Eskie. This is a last resort and should only be done in extreme circumstances. Some misguided owners feel they are doing their dog a service by shaving the Eskie's coat in summer, when exactly the opposite is true. The Eskie's coat serves as insulation against both heat and cold.

SOAP IT UP

The use of human soap products like shampoo, bubble bath and hand soap can be damaging to a dog's coat and skin. Human products are too strong; they remove the protective oils coating the dog's hair and skin that make him water-resistant. Use only shampoo made especially for dogs. You may like to use a medicated shampoo, which will help to keep external parasites at bay.

BATHING BEAUTY

Once you are sure that the dog is thoroughly rinsed, squeeze the excess water out of his coat with your hand and dry him with an heavy towel. Finish the job by using a blow dryer on the lowest heat setting. In cold weather, never allow your dog outside with a wet coat.

There are "dry bath" products on the market, which are sprays and powders intended for spot cleaning, that can be used between regular baths if necessary. They are not substitutes for regular baths, but they are easy to use for touch-ups as they do not require rinsing.

BATHING

Dogs do not need to be bathed as often as humans, but bathing as needed is essential for healthy skin and a clean, sparkling white coat. Again, like most anything, if you accustom your pup to being bathed as a puppy, it will be second nature by the time he grows up. You want your dog to be at ease in the bath or else it could end up a wet, soapy, messy ordeal for both of you!

Brush your American Eskimo thoroughly before wetting his coat. This will get rid of most mats and tangles, which are harder to remove when the coat is wet. Make certain that your dog has a good non-slip surface on which to stand. Begin by wetting the dog's coat, checking the water temperature to make sure that it is neither too hot nor too cold for the dog. A shower or hose attachment is necessary for thoroughly wetting and rinsing the coat.

Next, apply shampoo to the dog's coat and work it into a good lather. Wash the head last, as you do not want shampoo to drip into the dog's eyes while you are washing the rest of his body. You should use only a shampoo that is made for dogs. Do not use a product made for human hair. Work the shampoo all the way down to the skin. You can use this opportunity to check the skin for any bumps, bites or other abnormalities. Do not neglect any area of the

body—get all of the hard-to-reach places.

Once the dog has been thoroughly shampooed, he requires an equally thorough rinsing. Shampoo left in the coat can be irritating to the dog's skin. Protect his eyes from the shampoo by shielding them with your hand and directing the flow of water in the opposite direction. You also should avoid getting water in the ear canal. Be prepared for your dog to shake out his coat—you might want to stand back, but make sure you have a hold on the dog to keep him from running through the house.

Have a heavy towel on hand to remove much of the moisture from the Eskie's coat, and you may finish drying him with a blow dryer on the lowest setting or a blaster, which gives a stream of air but no heat.

EAR CLEANING

The ears should be kept clean with a cotton ball and ear-cleaning powder or liquid made especially for dogs. Do not probe into the ear canal with a cotton swab or anything else, as this can cause injury. Be on the lookout for any signs of infection or ear-mite infestation. If your Eskie has been shaking his head or scratching at his ears frequently, this usually indicates a problem. If the dog's ears have an unusual odor, this is

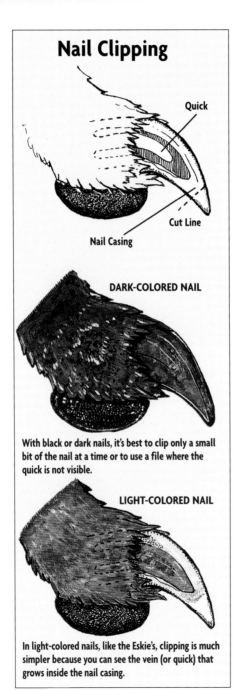

Nail Clipping

Quick

Cut Line

Nail Casing

DARK-COLORED NAIL

With black or dark nails, it's best to clip only a small bit of the nail at a time or to use a file where the quick is not visible.

LIGHT-COLORED NAIL

In light-colored nails, like the Eskie's, clipping is much simpler because you can see the vein (or quick) that grows inside the nail casing.

a sure sign of mite infestation or infection, and a signal to have his ears checked by the vet.

NAIL CLIPPING

During your grooming routine is the best time to accustom your Eskie to having his nails trimmed and his feet inspected. Always inspect your dog's feet for cracked pads. Check between the toes for splinters and thorns. Pay particular attention to any swollen or tender areas.

The nails of an Eskie who spends most of his time indoors or on grass when outdoors can grow long very quickly. Do not allow the nails to become overgrown and then expect to cut them back easily. Each nail has a blood vessel running through the center called the "quick." The quick grows close to the end of the nail and contains very sensitive nerve endings. If the nail is allowed to grow too long, it will be impossible to cut it back to a proper length without cutting into the quick. This causes severe pain to the dog and can also result in a great deal of bleeding that can be very difficult to stop.

If your Eskie is getting plenty of exercise on cement or rough hard pavement, the nails may be kept sufficiently worn down. Otherwise, the nails can grow long very quickly and must then be trimmed with canine nail clippers, an electric nail grinder (also called a drummel) or a coarse file made expressly for that purpose. All three of these items can be purchased at pet stores. Regardless of which nail-trimming device is used, proceed with caution and remove only a small portion of the nail at a time.

Should the quick be nipped in the trimming process, there are a number of blood-clotting products (such as styptic powder or pencil, as used for shaving) available at pet shops that will almost immediately stem the flow of blood. It is wise to have one of these products on hand in case there is a nail-trimming accident or the dog tears a nail on his own.

TRAVELING WITH YOUR DOG

CAR TRAVEL

You should accustom your American Eskimo to riding in a car at an early age. You may or may not take him in the car often, but at the very least he will need to go to the vet and you do not want these trips to be traumatic for the dog or troublesome for you. The safest way for a dog to ride in the car is in his crate. If he uses a crate in the house, you can use the same crate for travel.

Put the pup in the crate and see how he reacts. If he seems uneasy, you can have a passenger hold him on his lap while you drive. Another option for car travel is a specially made safety

PEDICURE TIP
A dog that spends a lot of time outside on a hard surface, such as cement or pavement, will have his nails naturally worn down and may not need to have them trimmed as often, except maybe in the colder months when he is not outside as much. Regardless, it is best to get your dog accustomed to the nail-trimming procedure at an early age so that he is used to it. Some dogs are especially sensitive about having their feet touched, but if a dog has experienced it since puppyhood, it should not bother him.

harness for dogs, which straps the dog in much like a seat belt. Do not let the dog roam loose in the vehicle—this is very dangerous! If you should stop short, your dog can be thrown and injured. If the dog starts climbing on you and pestering you while you are driving, you will not be able to concentrate on the road. It is an unsafe situation for everyone—human and canine.

For long trips, be prepared to stop to let the dog relieve himself. Take with you whatever you need to clean up after him, including some paper towels and perhaps some old rags or bath towels for use should he have a potty accident in the car or suffer from motion sickness.

Remember that no dog should ever be left in a car in hot weather. Temperatures can soar in a matter of minutes and your Eskie can die of heat exhaustion in less time than you would ever imagine. Rolling down the windows helps little and is dangerous in that an overheated

dog will panic and attempt to escape through the open window. A word to the wise—leave your Eskie at home in a cool room on hot days.

AIR TRAVEL

Contact your chosen airline before proceeding with your travel plans that include your American Eskimo Dog. The dog will be required to travel in a fiberglass crate and you should always check in advance with the airline regarding specific requirements for the crate's size, type and labeling, as well as any health certification needed for the dog or any travel restrictions. On many airlines, small pets whose crates fall within the specified size limitations are granted "carry-on" status and can accompany their owners in the cabin. This may be possible with the smaller Eskies; again, check with the airline ahead of time.

To help put the dog at ease, give him one of his favorite toys in the crate. Feed the dog a light meal several hours prior to checking in so that you minimize his need to relieve himself. For long trips, you will have to include food and water bowls to the outside of the dog's crate, so that airline employees can tend to the dogs between legs of the trip if he is not with you in the cabin.

Make sure that your Eskie is properly identified and that your

Your Eskie should always have his identification tag securely attached to his everyday collar, especially when outdoors or traveling.

contact information appears on his ID tags and on his crate. If not permitted in the cabin, your American Eskimo will travel in a different area of the plane than human passengers, so every rule must be strictly followed to prevent your dog's getting separated from you.

VACATIONS AND BOARDING

So you want to take a family vacation—and you want to include *all* members of the family. You would probably make arrangements for accommodations ahead of time anyway, but this is especially important when traveling with a dog. You do not want to make an overnight stop at the only place around for miles, only to find out that they do not allow dogs. Also,

you do not want to reserve a place for your family without confirming that you are traveling with a dog, because, if it is against the hotel's policy, you may end up without a place to stay.

Alternatively, if you are traveling and choose not to bring your American Eskimo, you will have to make arrangements for him while you are away. Some options are to take him to a friend's house to stay while you are gone, to have a trusted friend stop by often or stay at your house or to bring your dog to a reputable boarding kennel. If you choose to board him at a kennel, you should visit in advance to see the facilities provided and where the dogs are kept. Are the dogs' areas spacious and kept clean? Talk to some of

The light skin on the American Eskimo's belly and inner thigh are ideal places for a tattoo, as the tattoo will be easily visible.

the employees and observe how they treat the dogs—do they spend time with the dogs, play with them, exercise them, groom them, etc.? Also find out the kennel's policy on vaccinations and what they require. This is for all of the dogs' safety, since there is a greater risk of diseases being passed from dog to dog when dogs are kept together.

IDENTIFICATION

Your American Eskimo is your valued companion and friend. That is why you always keep a close eye on him and you have made sure that he cannot escape from the yard or wriggle out of his collar and run away from you. However, accidents can happen and there may come a time when your dog unexpectedly becomes separated from you. If this unfortunate event should occur, the first thing on your mind will be finding him. Proper identification, including an ID tag, and possibly a tattoo and/or microchip, will increase the chances of his being returned to you quickly and safely.

IDENTIFICATION OPTIONS

As puppies become more and more expensive, especially those puppies of high quality for showing and/or breeding, they have a greater chance of being stolen. The usual collar dog tag is, of course, easily removed. But there are two more permanent techniques that have become widely used for identifying dogs.

The puppy microchip implantation involves the injection of a small microchip, about the size of a corn kernel, under the skin of the dog. If your dog shows up at a clinic or shelter, or is offered for resale under less-than-savory circumstances, it can be positively identified by the microchip. The microchip is scanned, and a registry quickly identifies you as the owner.

Tattooing is done on various parts of the dog, from his belly to his ears. The number tattooed can be your telephone number, the dog's registration number or any other number that you can easily memorize. When professional dog thieves see a tattooed dog, they usually lose interest. For the safety of our dogs, no laboratory facility or dog broker will accept a tattooed dog as stock.

Discuss microchipping and tattooing with your vet and breeder. Some vets perform these services on their own premises for a reasonable fee. To ensure that the dog's ID is effective, be certain that the dog is then properly registered with a legitimate national database.

The leash, collar and ID tags are required accessories anytime you are out with your Eskie. Your dog should become accustomed to a light leash and collar as a youngster.

TRAINING YOUR

AMERICAN ESKIMO DOG

Living with an untrained dog is a lot like owning a piano that you do not know how to play—it is a nice object to look at, but it does not do much more than that to bring you pleasure. Now try taking piano lessons, and suddenly the piano comes alive and brings forth magical sounds and rhythms that set your heart singing and your body swaying.

The same is true with your American Eskimo Dog. Any dog is a big responsibility and, if not trained sensibly, may develop unacceptable behavior that annoys you or could even cause family friction.

To train your American Eskimo, you may like to enroll in an obedience class. Teach your dog good manners as you learn how and why he behaves the way he does. Find out how to communicate with your dog and how to recognize and understand his communications with you. Suddenly the dog takes on a new role in your life—he is clever, interesting, well behaved and fun to be with. He demonstrates his bond of devotion to you daily. In other words, your American

Eskimo does wonders for your ego because he constantly reminds you that you are not only his leader, you are his hero!

Those involved with teaching dog obedience and counseling owners about their dogs' behavior have discovered some interesting facts about dog ownership. For example, training dogs when they are puppies results in the highest rate of success in developing well-mannered and well-adjusted adult dogs. Training an older dog, from six months to six years of age, can produce almost equal results, providing that the owner accepts the dog's slower rate of learning capability and is willing to work patiently to help the dog succeed at developing to his fullest potential. Unfortunately, many owners

PARENTAL GUIDANCE
Training a dog is a life experience. Many parents admit that much of what they know about raising children they learned from caring for their dogs. Dogs respond to love, fairness and guidance, just as children do. Become a good dog owner and you may become an even better parent.

of untrained adult dogs lack the patience factor, so they do not persist until their dogs are successful at learning particular behaviors.

Training a puppy aged 10 to 16 weeks (20 weeks at the most) is like working with a dry sponge in a pool of water. The pup soaks up whatever you show him and constantly looks for more things to do and learn. At this early age, his body is not yet producing hormones, and therein lies the reason for such a high rate of success. Without hormones, the pup is focused on his owners and not particularly interested in investigating other places, dogs, people, etc. You are his leader: his provider of food, water, shelter and security. He latches onto you and wants to stay close. He will usually follow you from room to room, will not let you out of his sight when you are outdoors with him and will respond in like manner to the people and animals you encounter. If you greet a friend warmly, he will be happy to greet the person as well. If, however, you are hesitant or anxious about the approach of a stranger, he will respond accordingly.

Once the puppy begins to produce hormones, his natural curiosity emerges and he begins to investigate the world around him. It is at this time when you may notice that the untrained dog

REAP THE REWARDS

If you start with a normal, healthy dog and give him time, patience and some carefully executed lessons, you will reap the rewards of that training for the life of the dog. And what a life it will be! The two of you will find immeasurable pleasure in the companionship you have built together with love, respect and understanding.

begins to wander away from you and even ignore your commands to stay close. When this behavior becomes a problem, you have two choices: get rid of the dog or train him. It is strongly urged that you choose the latter option.

You usually will be able to find obedience classes within a reasonable distance from your home, but you can also do a lot to train your dog yourself. Sometimes there are classes available, but the tuition is too costly. Whatever the circumstances, the solution to training your dog without formal obedience classes lies within the pages of this book.

This chapter is devoted to helping you train your American Eskimo Dog at home. If the recommended procedures are followed faithfully, you may expect positive results that will prove rewarding both to you and your dog.

Whether your new charge is a puppy or a mature adult, the

methods of teaching and the techniques we use in training basic behaviors are the same. After all, no dog, whether puppy or adult, likes harsh or inhumane methods. All creatures, however, respond favorably to gentle motivational methods and sincere praise and encouragement. Now let us get started.

HOUSEBREAKING

You can train a puppy to relieve himself wherever you choose, but this must be somewhere suitable. You should bear in mind from the outset that when your puppy is old enough to go out in public places, any canine deposits must be removed at once. You will always have to carry with you a small plastic bag or "poop-scoop."

Outdoor training includes such surfaces as grass, soil and cement. Indoor training usually means training your dog to newspaper. When deciding on the surface and location that you will want your Eskie to use, be sure it is going to be permanent. Training your dog to grass and then changing your mind a few months later is extremely difficult for both dog and owner.

Next, choose the command you will use each and every time you want your puppy to void. "Hurry up" and "Let's go" are examples of commands commonly used by dog owners. Get in the habit of giving the

MEALTIME
Mealtime should be a peaceful time for your puppy. Do not put his food and water bowls in a high-traffic area in the house. For example, give him his own little corner of the kitchen where he can eat undisturbed and where he will not be underfoot. Do not allow small children or other family members to disturb the pup when he is eating.

HOW MANY TIMES A DAY?

AGE	RELIEF TRIPS
To 14 weeks	10
14–22 weeks	8
22–32 weeks	6
Adulthood	4
(dog stops growing)	

These are estimates, of course, but they are a guide to the *minimum* number of opportunities a dog should have each day to relieve himself.

The older the puppy, the less often he will need to relieve himself. Finally, as a mature healthy adult, he will require only three to five relief trips per day.

HOUSING

Since the types of housing and control you provide for your puppy have a direct relationship on the success of housebreaking, we consider the various aspects of both before we begin training.

Taking a new puppy home

Leash training goes hand in hand with house-training. Keep the puppy focused and interested in his lessons.

puppy your chosen relief command before you take him out. That way, when he becomes an adult, you will be able to determine if he wants to go out when you ask him. A confirmation will be signs of interest, such as wagging his tail, watching you intently, going to the door, etc.

PUPPY'S NEEDS

Your puppy needs to relieve himself after play periods, after each meal, after he has been sleeping and at any time he indicates that he is looking for a place to urinate or defecate. The urinary and intestinal tract muscles of very young puppies are not fully developed. Therefore, like human babies, puppies need to relieve themselves frequently.

Take your puppy out often—every hour for an eight-week-old, for example—and always immediately after sleeping and eating.

CANINE DEVELOPMENT SCHEDULE

It is important to understand how and at what age a puppy develops into adulthood.
If you are a puppy owner, consult the following Canine Development Schedule to
determine the stage of development your puppy is currently experiencing.
This knowledge will help you as you work with the puppy in the weeks and months ahead.

Period	Age	Characteristics
First to Third	**Birth to Seven Weeks**	Puppy needs food, sleep and warmth, and responds to simple and gentle touching. Needs mother for security and disciplining. Needs littermates for learning and interacting with other dogs. Pup learns to function within a pack and learns pack order of dominance. Begin socializing pup with adults and children for short periods. Pup begins to become aware of his environment.
Fourth	**Eight to Twelve Weeks**	Brain is fully developed. Needs socializing with outside world. Remove from mother and littermates. Needs to change from canine pack to human pack. Human dominance necessary. Fear period occurs between 8 and 12 weeks. Avoid fright and pain.
Fifth	**Thirteen to Sixteen Weeks**	Training and formal obedience should begin. Less association with other dogs, more with people, places, situations. Period will pass easily if you remember this is pup's change-to-adolescence time. Be firm and fair. Flight instinct prominent. Permissiveness and over-disciplining can do permanent damage. Praise for good behavior.
Juvenile	**Four to Eight Months**	Another fear period about 7 to 8 months of age. It passes quickly, but be cautious of fright and pain. Sexual maturity reached. Dominant traits established. Dog should understand sit, down, come and stay by now.

NOTE: THESE ARE APPROXIMATE TIME FRAMES. ALLOW FOR INDIVIDUAL DIFFERENCES IN PUPPIES.

COMMAND STANCE
Stand up straight and authoritatively when giving your dog commands. Do not issue commands when lying on the floor or lying on your back on the sofa. If you are on your hands and knees when you give a command, your dog will think you are positioning yourself to play.

and turning him loose in your house can be compared to turning a child loose in an amusement park and telling the child that the place is all his! The sheer enormity of the place would be too much for him to handle. Instead, offer the puppy clearly defined areas where he can play, sleep, eat and live. A room of the house where the family gathers is the most obvious choice. Puppies are social animals and need to feel a part of the pack right from the start. Hearing your voice, watching you while you are doing things and smelling you nearby are all positive reinforcers that he is now a member of your pack. Usually a family room, the kitchen or a nearby adjoining breakfast area is ideal for providing safety and security for both puppy and owner.

Within the designated room, there should be a smaller area that the puppy can call his own. An alcove, a wire or fiberglass dog crate or a partitioned (not boarded!) corner from which he can view the activities of his new family will be fine. The size of the area or crate is the key factor here. The area must be large enough so that the puppy can lie down and stretch out, as well as stand up, without rubbing his head on the top. At the same time, it must be small enough so that he cannot relieve himself at one end and sleep at the other without coming into contact with his droppings during the housebreaking process. Dogs are, by nature, clean animals and will not remain close to their relief areas unless forced to do so. In those cases, they then become dirty dogs and usually remain that way for life.

The dog's designated area should contain clean bedding and a toy. Avoid putting food or water in the dog's crate before he is fully housebroken, as eating and drinking will activate his digestive

Don't miss the signals your dog gives you when he has to go out…or wants to come back in!

processes and ultimately defeat your purpose, not to mention make the puppy very uncomfortable if he always has "to go." Once housebreaking has been achieved reliably, water should always be available in his area, in a non-spill container.

CONTROL

By *control*, we mean helping the puppy to create a lifestyle pattern that will be compatible to that of his human pack (*you*!). Just as we guide little children to learn our way of life, we must show the puppy when it is time to play, eat,

THE SUCCESS METHOD

Success that comes by luck is usually short-lived. Success that comes by well-thought-out proven methods is often more easily achieved and permanent. This is the Success Method. It is designed to give you, the puppy owner, a simple yet proven way to help your puppy develop clean living habits and a feeling of security in his new environment.

6 Steps to Successful Crate Training

1 Tell the puppy "Crate time!" and place him in the crate with a small treat (a piece of cheese or half of a biscuit). Let him stay in the crate for five minutes while you are in the same room. Then release him and praise lavishly. Never release him when he is fussing. Wait until he is quiet before you let him out.

2 Repeat Step 1 several times a day.

3 The next day, place the puppy in the crate as before. Let him stay there for ten minutes. Do this several times.

4 Continue building time in five-minute increments until the puppy stays in his crate for 30 minutes with you in the room. Always take him to his relief area after prolonged periods in his crate.

5 Now go back to Step 1 and let the puppy stay in his crate for five minutes, this time while you are out of the room.

6 Once again, build crate time in five-minute increments with you out of the room. When the puppy will stay willingly in his crate (he may even fall asleep!) for 30 minutes with you out of the room, he will be ready to stay in it for several hours at a time.

sleep, exercise and even entertain himself.

Your puppy should always sleep in his crate. He should also learn that, during times of household confusion and excessive human activity, such as at breakfast when family members are preparing for the day, he can play by himself in relative safety and comfort in his designated area. Each time you leave the puppy alone, he should understand exactly where he is to stay.

Puppies are chewers. They cannot tell the difference between lamp cords, television wires, shoes, table legs, etc. Chewing into a television cord, for example, can be fatal to the puppy, while a shorted wire can start a fire in the house. If the puppy chews on the arm of the chair when he is alone, you will probably discipline him angrily when you get home. Thus, he makes the association that your coming home means he is going to be punished. (He will not remember chewing the chair and is incapable of making the association of the discipline with his naughty deed.) Accustoming the pup to his designated area not only keeps him safe but also avoids his engaging in destructive behaviors when you are not around.

Times of excitement, such as special occasions, family parties, etc., can be fun for the puppy, providing that he can view the

Always clean up after your dog, whether you are in public or your own backyard.

activities from the security of his designated area. He is not underfoot and he is not being fed all sorts of tidbits that will probably cause him stomach distress, yet he still feels a part of the fun.

ESTABLISHING A SCHEDULE

A puppy should be taken to his relief area each time he is released from his designated area, after meals, after play sessions and when he first awakens in the morning (at age 8–10 weeks, this can mean 5 a.m.!). The puppy will indicate that he's ready "to go" by circling or sniffing busily—do not misinterpret these signs. For a puppy less than ten weeks of age, a routine of taking him out every hour is necessary. As the puppy grows, he will be able to wait for longer periods of time.

Keep trips to his relief area short. Stay no more than five or six minutes and then return to the house. If he goes during that time, praise him lavishly and take him indoors immediately. If he does

More than one pup per crate is acceptable for travel, but for housebreaking purposes, each pup must have an individual crate that is a place of his own.

tiate between the times for play versus the times for relief. Help him develop regular hours for naps, being alone, playing by himself and just resting, all in his crate. Encourage him to entertain himself while you are busy with your activities. Let him learn that having you near is comforting, but it is not your main purpose in life to provide him with undivided attention. Each time you put your puppy in his own area, use the same command, whatever suits best. Soon he will run to his crate or special area when he hears you say those words.

Crate training provides safety for you, the puppy and the home. It also provides the puppy with a feeling of security, and that helps the puppy achieve self-confidence and clean habits. Remember that one of the primary ingredients in housebreaking your puppy is

not, but he has an accident when you go back indoors, pick him up immediately, say "No! No!" and return to his relief area. Wait a few minutes, then return to the house again. Never hit a puppy or put his face in urine or excrement when he has had an accident!

Once indoors, put the puppy in his crate until you have had time to clean up his accident. Then, release him to the family area and watch him more closely than before. Chances are, his accident was a result of your not picking up his signal or waiting too long before offering him the opportunity to relieve himself. Never hold a grudge against the puppy for accidents.

Let the puppy learn that going outdoors means it is time to relieve himself, not to play. Once trained, he will be able to play indoors and out and still differen-

THE CLEAN LIFE

By providing sleeping and resting quarters that fit the dog, and offering frequent opportunities to relieve himself outside his quarters, the puppy quickly learns that the outdoors (or the newspaper if you are training him to paper) is the place to go when he needs to urinate or defecate. It also reinforces his innate desire to keep his sleeping quarters clean. This, in turn, helps develop the muscle control that will eventually produce a dog with clean living habits.

control. Regardless of your lifestyle, there will always be occasions when you will need to have a place where your dog can stay and be happy and safe. Crate training is the answer for now and in the future.

In conclusion, a few key elements are really all you need for a successful housebreaking method—consistency, frequency, praise, control and supervision. By following these procedures with a normal, healthy puppy, you and the puppy will soon be past the stage of "accidents" and ready to move on to a clean and rewarding life together.

ROLES OF DISCIPLINE, REWARD AND PUNISHMENT

Discipline, training one to act in accordance with rules, brings order to life. It is as simple as that. Without discipline, particularly in a group society, chaos will reign supreme and the group will eventually perish. Humans and canines are social animals and need some form of discipline in order to function effectively. They must procure food, reproduce to keep their species going and protect their home base and their young. If there were no discipline in the lives of social animals, they would eventually die from starvation and/or predation by other stronger animals. In the case of domestic canines, discipline in their lives is needed in order for

them to understand how their pack (you and other family members) functions and how they must act in order to survive.

A large humane society in a highly populated area recently surveyed dog owners regarding their satisfaction with their relationships with their dogs. People who had trained their dogs were

CALM DOWN

Dogs will do anything for your attention. If you reward the dog when he is calm and attentive, you will develop a well-mannered dog. If, on the other hand, you greet your dog excitedly and encourage him to wrestle with you, the dog will greet you the same way and you will have a hyperactive dog on your hands.

75% more satisfied with their pets than those who had never trained their dogs.

Dr. Edward Thorndike, a noted psychologist, established *Thorndike's Theory of Learning*, which states that a behavior that results in a pleasant event tends to be repeated. Furthermore, it concludes that a behavior that results in an unpleasant event tends not to be repeated. It is this theory upon which training methods are based today. For example, if you manipulate a dog to perform a specific behavior and reward him for doing it, he is likely to do it again because he enjoyed the end result.

Occasionally, punishment, a penalty inflicted for an offense, is necessary. The best type of punishment often comes from an outside source. For example, a child is told not to touch the stove because he may get burned. He disobeys and touches the stove. In doing so, he receives a burn. From that time on, he respects the heat of the stove and avoids contact with it. Therefore, a behavior that results in an unpleasant event tends not to be repeated.

A good example of a dog's learning the hard way is the dog who chases the house cat. He is told many times to leave the cat alone, yet he persists in teasing the cat. Then, one day, the dog begins chasing the cat but the cat turns and swipes a claw across the dog's face, leaving the dog with a painful gash on his nose. The final result is that the dog stops chasing the cat.

TRAINING EQUIPMENT

COLLAR AND LEASH
For an American Eskimo Dog, the collar and leash that you use for training must be one with which you are easily able to work, not too heavy for the dog and perfectly safe.

TREATS
Have a bag of treats on hand; something nutritious and easy to swallow works best. Use a soft treat, a chunk of cheese or a piece of cooked chicken rather than a dry biscuit. By the time the dog has finished chewing a dry treat, he will forget why he is being rewarded in the first place!

Using food rewards will not teach a dog to beg at the table— the only way to teach a dog to beg at the table is to give him food from the table. In training, rewarding the dog with a food treat will help him associate praise and the treats with learning new behaviors that obviously please his owner.

TRAINING BEGINS: ASK THE DOG A QUESTION
In order to teach your dog anything, you must first get his attention. After all, he cannot

learn anything if he is looking away from you with his mind on something else.

To get your dog's attention, ask him "School?" and immediately walk over to him and give him a treat as you tell him "Good dog." Wait a minute or two and repeat the routine, this time with a treat in your hand as you approach within a foot of the dog. Do not go directly to him, but stop about a foot short of him and hold out the treat as you ask "School?" He will see you approaching with a treat in your hand and most likely begin walking toward you. As you meet, give him the treat and praise again.

The third time, ask the ques-tion, have a treat in your hand and walk only a short distance toward the dog so that he must walk almost all the way to you. As he reaches you, give him the treat and praise again.

By this time, the dog will probably be getting the idea that if he pays attention to you, especially when you ask that question, it will pay off in treats and enjoy-able activities for him. In other words, he learns that "school" means doing great things with you that are fun and that result in positive attention for him.

Remember that the dog does not understand your verbal language; he only recognizes sounds. Your question translates

Consider the abundant coat around your Eskie's neck when choosing a collar. Make sure it is appropriately sized and made of a material that will not damage the coat.

bend his knees to maintain his balance. As he bends his knees, he will assume a sit position. At that point, release the food treat and praise lavishly with comments such as "Good dog! Good sit!," etc. Remember to always praise enthusiastically, because dogs relish verbal praise from their owners and feel so proud of themselves whenever they accomplish a behavior.

You will not use food forever in getting the dog to obey your commands. Food is only used to teach new behaviors and, once the dog knows what you want when you give a specific command, you will wean him off the food treats but still maintain the verbal praise. After all, you will always have your voice with you, and there will be many times when you have no food rewards but expect the dog to obey.

Training your Eskie to sit upon command is the first exercise you should attempt. It is easy for the dog to learn and will serve as a basis for other exercises.

to a series of sounds for him, and those sounds become the signal to go to you and pay attention. The dog learns that if he does this, he will get to interact with you plus receive treats and praise.

THE BASIC COMMANDS

TEACHING SIT
Now that you have the dog's attention, attach his leash and hold it in your left hand, and hold a food treat in your right hand. Place your food hand at the dog's nose and let him lick the treat but not take it from you. Say "Sit" and slowly raise your food hand from in front of the dog's nose up over his head so that he is looking at the ceiling. As he bends his head upward, he will have to

TEACHING DOWN
Teaching the down exercise is easy when you understand how the dog perceives the down position, and it is very difficult when you do not. Dogs perceive the down position as a submissive one; therefore, teaching the down exercise by using a forceful method can sometimes make the dog develop such a fear of the down that he either runs away when you say "Down" or he attempts to snap at the person who tries to force him down.

Have the dog sit close alongside your left leg, facing in the same direction as you are. Hold the leash in your left hand and a food treat in your right. Now place your left hand lightly on the top of the dog's shoulders where they meet above the spinal cord. Do not push down on the dog's shoulders; simply rest your left hand there so you can guide the dog to lie down close to your left leg rather than to swing away from your side when he drops.

Now place the food hand at the dog's nose, say "Down" very softly (almost a whisper) and slowly lower the food hand to the dog's front feet. When the food hand reaches the floor, begin moving it forward along the floor in front of the dog. Keep talking softly to the dog, saying things like, "Do you want this treat? You can do this, good dog." Your reassuring tone of voice will help calm the dog as he tries to follow the food hand in order to get the treat.

When the dog's elbows touch the floor, release the food and praise softly. Try to get the dog to maintain the down position for several seconds before you let him sit up. The goal here is to get the dog to settle down and not feel threatened in the down position.

TEACHING STAY

It is easy to teach the dog to stay in either a sit or a down position.

Again, we use food and praise during the teaching process as we help the dog to understand exactly what it is that we are expecting him to do.

To teach the sit/stay, start with the dog sitting on your left side as before and hold the leash in your left hand. Have a food treat in your right hand and place your food hand at the dog's nose. Say "Stay" and step out on your right foot to stand directly in front of the dog, toe to toe, as he licks and nibbles the treat. Be sure to keep his head facing upward to main-

DOUBLE JEOPARDY

A dog in jeopardy never lies down. He stays alert on his feet because instinct tells him that he may have to run away or fight for his survival. Therefore, if a dog feels threatened or anxious, he will not lie down. Consequently, it is important to keep the dog calm and relaxed as he learns the down exercise.

Handlers in the show ring use bits of food to encourage their dogs to stay in the standing position. As the dog focuses on the treat and stands at attention, he looks his best for the judge.

you do, use your left hand open with the palm facing the dog as a stay signal, much the same as the hand signal a police officer uses to stop traffic at an intersection. Hold the food treat in your right hand as before, but this time the food will not be touching the dog's nose. He will watch the food hand and quickly learn that he is going to get that treat as soon as you return to his side.

When you can stand 3 feet away from your dog for 30 seconds, you can then begin building time and distance in both stays. Eventually, the dog can be expected to remain in the stay position for prolonged periods of time until you return to him or call him to you. Always praise lavishly when he stays.

tain the sit position. Count to five and then swing around to stand next to the dog again with him on your left. As soon as you get back to the original position, release the food and praise lavishly.

To teach the down/stay, do the down as previously described. As soon as the dog lies down, say "Stay" and step out on your right foot just as you did in the sit/stay. Count to five and then return to stand beside the dog with him on your left side. Release the treat and praise as always.

Within a week or ten days, you can begin to add a bit of distance between you and your dog when you leave him. When

CONSISTENCY PAYS OFF

Dogs need consistency in their feeding schedule, exercise and relief visits, and in the verbal commands you use. If you use "Stay" on Monday and "Stay here, please" on Tuesday, you will confuse your dog. Don't demand perfect behavior during training sessions and then let him have the run of the house the rest of the day. Above all, lavish praise on your pet consistently every time he does something right. The more he feels he is pleasing you, the more willing he will be to learn.

"COME" . . . BACK

Never call your dog to come to you for a correction or scold him when he reaches you. That is the quickest way to turn a come command into "Go away fast!" Dogs think only in the present tense, and your dog will connect the scolding with coming to you, not with the misbehavior of a few moments earlier.

TEACHING COME

If you make teaching "come" an exciting experience, you should never have a "student" that does not love the game or that fails to come when called. The secret, it seems, is never to teach the word "come."

At times when an owner most wants his dog to come when called, the owner is likely to be upset or anxious and he allows these feelings to come through in the tone of his voice when he calls his dog. Hearing that desperation in his owner's voice, the dog fears the results of going to him and therefore either disobeys outright or runs in the opposite direction. The secret, therefore, is to teach the dog a game and, when you want him to come to you, simply play the game. It is practically a no-fail solution!

To begin, have several members of your family take a few food treats and each go into a different room in the house.

Everyone takes turns calling the dog, and each person should celebrate the dog's finding him with a treat and lots of happy praise. When a person calls the dog, he is actually inviting the dog to find him and to get a treat as a reward for "winning."

A few turns of the "Where are you?" game and the dog will understand that everyone is playing the game and that each person has a big celebration awaiting the dog's success at locating him or her. Once the dog learns to love the game, simply calling out "Where are you?" will bring him running from wherever he is when he hears that all-important question.

The come command is recognized as one of the most important things to teach a dog, but there are trainers who work with thousands of dogs and never use the actual word "come." Yet these dogs will race to respond to a

Minimize the distractions in your training area. It's hard to have a successful lesson if your dog is paying attention to other things.

HEELING WELL

Teach your dog to heel in an enclosed area. Once you think the dog will obey reliably and you want to attempt advanced obedience exercises such as off-leash heeling, test him in a fenced-in area so he cannot run away.

TEACHING HEEL

Heeling means that the dog walks beside the owner without pulling. It takes time and patience on the owner's part to succeed at teaching the dog that he (the owner) will not proceed unless the dog is walking calmly beside him. Neither pulling out ahead on the leash nor lagging behind is acceptable.

Begin by holding the leash in your left hand as the dog sits beside your left leg. Move the loop end of the leash to your right hand, but keep your left hand short on the leash so that it keeps the dog in close next to you.

Say "Heel" and step forward on your left foot. Keep the dog close to you and take three steps. Stop and have the dog sit next to you in what we now call the heel position. Praise verbally, but do not touch the dog. Hesitate a moment and begin again with "Heel," taking three steps and stopping, at which point the dog is told to sit again.

Your goal here is to have the dog walk those three steps without pulling on the leash. Once he will walk calmly beside you for three steps without pulling, increase the number of steps you take to five. When he will walk politely beside you while you take five steps, you can increase the length of your walk to ten steps. Keep increasing the length of your stroll until the dog will walk

person who uses the dog's name followed by "Where are you?" For example, a woman has a 12-year-old companion dog who went blind, but who never fails to locate her owner when asked, "Where are you?"

Children, in particular, love to play this game with their dogs. Children can hide in smaller places like a shower stall or bathtub, behind a bed or under a table. The dog needs to work a little bit harder to find these hiding places, but, when he does, he loves to celebrate with a treat and a tussle with a favorite youngster.

quietly beside you without pulling as long as you want him to heel. When you stop heeling, indicate to the dog that the exercise is over by verbally praising as you pet him and say, "OK, good dog." The "OK" is used as a release word, meaning that the exercise is finished and the dog is free to relax.

If you are dealing with a dog who insists on pulling you around, simply "put on your brakes" and stand your ground until the dog realizes that the two of you are not going anywhere until he is beside you and moving at your pace, not his. It may take some time just standing there to convince the dog that you are the leader and that you will be the one to decide on the direction and speed of your travel.

Each time the dog looks up at you or slows down to give a slack leash between the two of you, quietly praise him and say, "Good heel. Good dog." Eventually, the dog will begin to respond and within a few days he will be walking politely beside you without pulling on the leash. At first, the training sessions should be kept short and very positive; soon the dog will be able to walk nicely with you for increasingly longer distances. Remember also to give the dog free time and the opportunity to run and play when you have finished heel practice.

WEANING OFF FOOD IN TRAINING

Food is used in training new behaviors. Once the dog understands what behavior goes with a specific command, it is time to start weaning him off

FEAR AGGRESSION

Pups who are subjected to physical abuse during training commonly end up with behavioral problems as adults. One common result of abuse is fear aggression, in which a dog will lash out, bare his teeth, snarl and finally bite someone by whom he feels threatened. For example, your daughter may be playing with the dog one afternoon. As they play hide-and-seek, she backs the dog into a corner and, as she attempts to tease him playfully, he bites her hand. Examine the cause of this behavior. Did your daughter ever hit the dog? Did someone who resembles your daughter hit or scream at the dog?

Fortunately, fear aggression is relatively easy to correct. Have your daughter engage in only positive activities with the dog, such as feeding, petting and walking. She should not give any corrections or negative feedback. If the dog still growls or cowers away from her, allow someone else to accompany them. After approximately one week, the dog should feel that he can rely on her for many positive things, and he will also be prevented from reacting fearfully towards anyone who might resemble her.

SAFETY FIRST

While it may seem that the most important things to your dog are eating, sleeping and chewing the upholstery on your furniture, his first concern is actually safety. The domesticated dogs we keep as companions have the same pack instinct as their ancestors who ran free thousands of years ago. Because of this pack instinct, your dog wants to know that he and his pack are not in danger of being harmed, and that his pack has a strong, capable leader. You must establish yourself as the leader early on in your relationship. That way, your dog will trust that you will take care of him and the pack, and he will accept your commands without question.

the food treats. At first, give a treat after each exercise. Then, start to give a treat only after every other exercise. Mix up the times when you offer a food reward and the times when you only offer praise so that the dog will never know when he is going to receive both food and praise and when he is going to receive only praise. This is called a variable-ratio reward system. It proves successful because there is always the chance that the owner will produce a treat, so the dog never stops trying for that reward. No matter what, *always* give verbal praise.

OBEDIENCE CLASSES

It is a good idea to enroll in an obedience class if one is available in your area. If yours is a show dog, classes to prepare for the show ring would be more appropriate. Many areas have dog clubs that offer basic obedience training as well as preparatory classes for obedience competition. There are also local dog trainers who offer similar classes.

At obedience trials, dogs can earn titles at various levels of competition, and Eskies are very enthusiastic competitors. The beginning levels of obedience competition include basic behaviors such as sit, down, heel, etc. The more advanced levels of competition include jumping, retrieving, scent discrimination and signal work. The advanced levels require a dog and owner to put a lot of time and effort into their training. The titles that can be earned at these levels of competition are very prestigious.

OTHER ACTIVITIES FOR LIFE

Whether a dog is trained in the structured environment of a class or alone with his owner at home, there are many activities that can bring fun and rewards to both owner and dog once they have mastered basic control. American Eskimo Dogs are especially adaptive for Hearing Ear programs for the deaf, and they make excellent therapy dogs for hospitals and homes for the elderly.

Teaching the dog to help out around the home, in the yard or on the farm provides great satisfaction to both dog and owner. In addition, the dog's help makes life a little easier for his owner and raises his stature as a valued companion to his family. It helps give the dog a purpose by occupying his mind and providing an outlet for his energy.

Backpacking is an exciting and healthy activity that the dog can be taught without assistance from more than his owner. The exercise of walking and climbing is good for man and dog alike, and the bond that they develop together is priceless. The rule for backpacking with any dog is never to expect the dog to carry more than one-sixth of his body weight.

If you are interested in participating in organized competition with your Eskie,

KEEP SMILING

Never train your dog, puppy or adult, when you are angry or in a sour mood. Dogs are very sensitive to human feelings, especially anger, and if your dog senses that you are angry or upset, he will connect your anger with his training and learn to resent or fear his training sessions.

there are activities other than obedience in which you and your dog can become involved. Agility is a popular sport in which dogs run through obstacle courses that include various jumps, tunnels and other exercises to test the dog's speed and coordination. Again, as with obedience, the Eskie tackles agility with great enthusiasm. The owners run beside their dogs to give commands and to guide them through the course. Although competitive, the focus is on fun—it's fun to do, fun to watch and great exercise.

Within your Eskie lies a world of potential. Try different activities to find out what makes him happy, and go for it!

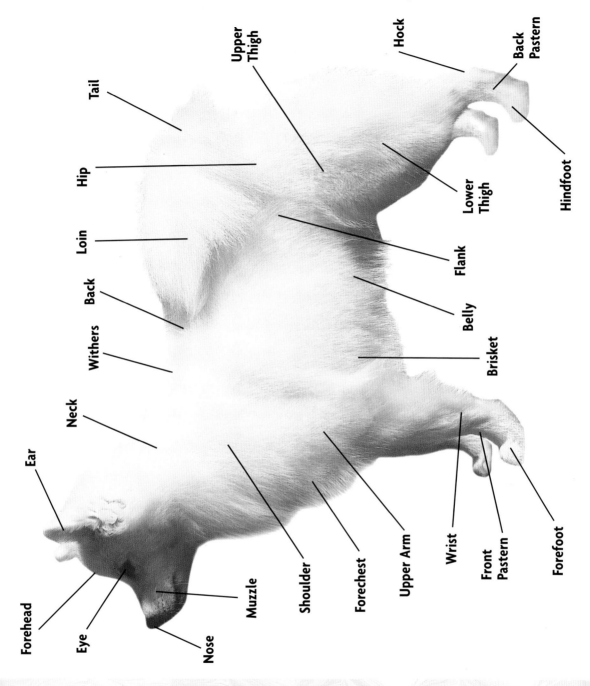

PHYSICAL STRUCTURE OF THE AMERICAN ESKIMO DOG

Dogs suffer from many of the same physical illnesses as people and might even share many of the same psychological problems. Since people usually know more about human diseases than canine maladies, many of the terms used in this chapter will be familiar but not necessarily those used by veterinarians. For example, we will use the familiar term *x-ray* instead of *radiograph*. We will also use the familiar term *symptoms*, even though dogs don't have symptoms, which are verbal descriptions of something the patient feels or observes himself that he regards as abnormal. Dogs have *clinical signs* since they cannot speak, so we have to look for these clinical signs...but we still use the term *symptoms* in the book.

Medicine is a constantly changing art, with some scientific input as well. Things alter as we learn more and more about basic sciences such as genetics and biochemistry, and have use of more sophisticated imaging techniques like Computer Aided Tomography (CAT scans) or Magnetic Resonance Imaging (MRI scans). There is academic dispute about many canine maladies, so different veterinarians treat them in different ways; for example, some vets place a greater emphasis on surgical treatment than others.

SELECTING A VETERINARIAN
Your selection of a veterinarian should be based on personal recommendation for his skills with small animals, especially dogs, and, if possible, especially American Eskimo Dogs or at least spitz breeds. If the vet is based nearby, it will be helpful because you might have an emergency or need to make multiple visits for treatments.

All veterinarians are licensed and should be capable of dealing with routine medical issues such as infections, injuries, routine surgeries and the promotion of health (for example, by vaccination). If the problem affecting your dog is more complex, your vet will refer your pet to someone with a more detailed knowledge of what is wrong. This will usually be a specialist at the nearest university veterinary school who concentrates in the field relevant to your

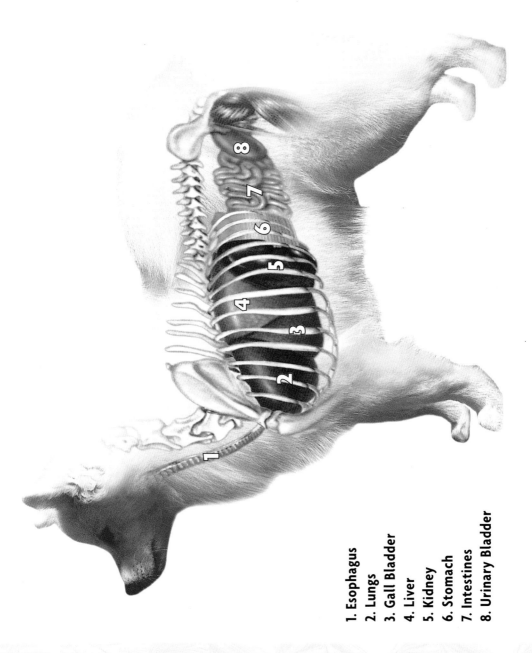

1. Esophagus
2. Lungs
3. Gall Bladder
4. Liver
5. Kidney
6. Stomach
7. Intestines
8. Urinary Bladder

INTERNAL ORGANS OF THE AMERICAN ESKIMO DOG

dog's problem (e.g., veterinary dermatology, veterinary ophthalmology, etc.).

Veterinary procedures are very costly and as the treatments available improve, they are going to become more expensive. It is quite acceptable to discuss matters of cost with your vet; if there is more than one treatment option, cost may be a factor in deciding which route to take. It is also acceptable to get a second opinion, but it is courteous to advise the vets concerned that you are doing so.

Insurance against veterinary cost is also becoming very popular. There are a range of policies available, the most extensive of which will cover routine health care, including check-ups, prescription flea prevention and the like.

PREVENTATIVE MEDICINE

It is much easier, less costly and more effective to practice preventative medicine than to fight bouts of illness and disease. Properly bred puppies of all breeds come from parents that were selected based upon their genetic-disease profiles. The puppies' mother should have been vaccinated, free of all internal and external parasites and properly nourished. For these reasons, a visit to the veterinarian who cared for the dam is recommended if at all possible. The dam passes disease resistance to her puppies, which should last

Breakdown of Veterinary Income by Category

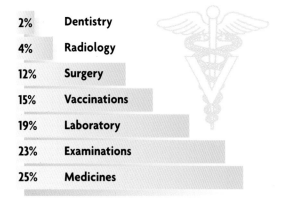

2%	Dentistry
4%	Radiology
12%	Surgery
15%	Vaccinations
19%	Laboratory
23%	Examinations
25%	Medicines

A typical vet's income, categorized according to services performed. This survey dealt with small-animal (pets) practices.

from eight to ten weeks. Unfortunately, she can also pass on parasites and infection. This is why knowledge about her health is useful in learning more about the health of the puppies.

WEANING TO FIVE MONTHS OLD

Puppies should be weaned by the time they are two months old. A puppy that remains for at least eight weeks with his mother and littermates usually adapts better to other dogs and people later in life.

Sometimes new owners have their puppy examined by a veterinarian immediately, which is a good idea unless the puppy is overtired by a long journey home from the breeder's. In that case, the appointment should be arranged for the day after bringing the pup home.

The puppy will have his teeth examined and his skeletal confor-

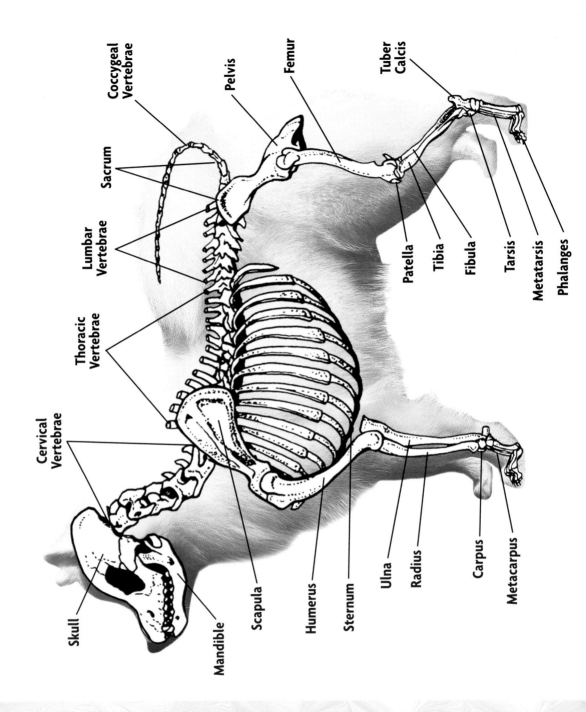

Coccygeal Vertebrae

Pelvis

Femur

Tuber Calcis

Sacrum

Lumbar Vertebrae

Patella

Tibia

Fibula

Tarsis

Metatarsis

Phalanges

Thoracic Vertebrae

Cervical Vertebrae

Skull

Mandible

Scapula

Humerus

Sternum

Ulna

Radius

Carpus

Metacarpus

SKELETAL STRUCTURE OF THE AMERICAN ESKIMO DOG

mation and general health checked prior to certification by the vet. Puppies in certain breeds have problems with their kneecaps, cataracts and other eye problems, heart murmurs and undescended testicles. If your vet has training in temperament evaluation, he may be able to evaluate your pup's personality. Also at the first visit, the vet will set up a schedule for the pup's vaccinations.

VACCINATIONS
Most vaccinations are given by injection and should only be given by a veterinarian. Both he and you should keep a record of the date of the injection, the identification of the vaccine and the amount given. Some vets give a first vaccination at six weeks, but some dog breeders prefer the course not to commence until about eight weeks because of the risk of interaction with the antibodies produced by the mother. The vaccination scheduling is usually based on a two- to four-week cycle. You must take your vet's advice as to when to vaccinate, as this may differ according to the vaccine used.

The usual vaccines contain immunizing doses of several different viruses such as distemper, parvovirus,

HEALTH AND VACCINATION SCHEDULE

AGE IN WEEKS:	6TH	8TH	10TH	12TH	14TH	16TH	20-24TH	52ND
Worm Control	✔	✔	✔	✔	✔	✔	✔	
Neutering							✔	
Heartworm		✔		✔		✔	✔	
Parvovirus	✔		✔		✔		✔	✔
Distemper		✔		✔		✔		✔
Hepatitis		✔		✔		✔		✔
Leptospirosis								✔
Parainfluenza	✔		✔		✔			✔
Dental Examination		✔					✔	✔
Complete Physical		✔					✔	✔
Coronavirus				✔			✔	✔
Canine Cough	✔							
Hip Dysplasia								✔
Rabies							✔	

Vaccinations are not instantly effective. It takes about two weeks for the dog's immune system to develop antibodies. Most vaccinations require annual booster shots. Your vet should guide you in this regard.

parainfluenza and hepatitis. There are other vaccines available when the puppy is at risk. You should rely upon professional advice. This is especially true for the booster immunizations. Most vaccination programs require a booster when the puppy is a year old and once a year thereafter. In some cases, circumstances may require more or less frequent immunizations.

Canine cough, more formally known as tracheobronchitis, is immunized against with a vaccine that is sprayed into the dog's nostrils. Canine cough is usually included in routine vaccination, but it is often not as effective as the vaccines for other major diseases.

FIVE MONTHS TO ONE YEAR OF AGE

Unless you intend to breed or show your dog, neutering the puppy is recommended. Good breeders sell pet-quality puppies on the condition that the owners have the pups neutered/spayed at the appropriate age, usually before or around six months of age. Discuss all aspects with your

Normal hairs of a dog enlarged 200 times original size. The cuticle (outer covering) is clean and healthy. Unlike human hair that grows from the base, a dog's hair also grows from the end. Damaged hairs and split ends, illustrated above.

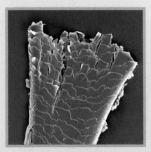
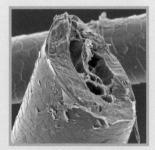
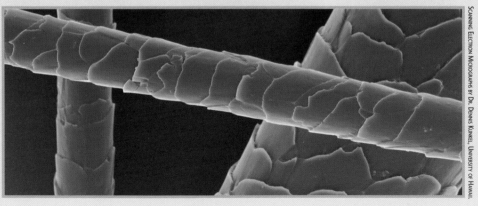

SCANNING ELECTRON MICROGRAPHS BY DR. DENNIS KUNKEL, UNIVERSITY OF HAWAII.

DISEASE REFERENCE CHART

	What is it?	What causes it?	Symptoms
Leptospirosis	Severe disease that affects the internal organs; can be spread to people.	A bacterium, which is often carried by rodents, that enters through mucous membranes and spreads quickly throughout the body.	Range from fever, vomiting and loss of appetite in less severe cases to shock, irreversible kidney damage and possibly death in most severe cases.
Rabies	Potentially deadly virus that infects warm-blooded mammals.	Bite from a carrier of the virus, mainly wild animals.	1st stage: dog exhibits change in behavior, fear. 2nd stage: dog's behavior becomes more aggressive. 3rd stage: loss of coordination, trouble with bodily functions.
Parvovirus	Highly contagious virus, potentially deadly.	Ingestion of the virus, which is usually spread through the feces of infected dogs.	Most common: severe diarrhea. Also vomiting, fatigue, lack of appetite.
Canine cough	Contagious respiratory infection.	Combination of types of bacteria and virus. Most common: *Bordetella bronchiseptica* bacteria and parainfluenza virus.	Chronic cough.
Distemper	Disease primarily affecting respiratory and nervous system.	Virus that is related to the human measles virus.	Mild symptoms such as fever, lack of appetite and mucus secretion progress to evidence of brain damage, "hard pad."
Hepatitis	Virus primarily affecting the liver.	Canine adenovirus type I (CAV-1). Enters system when dog breathes in particles.	Lesser symptoms include listlessness, diarrhea, vomiting. More severe symptoms include "blue-eye" (clumps of virus in eye).
Coronavirus	Virus resulting in digestive problems.	Virus is spread through infected dog's feces.	Stomach upset evidenced by lack of appetite, vomiting, diarrhea.

veterinarian. Neutering and spaying have proven to be extremely beneficial to male and female puppies, respectively. Besides eliminating the possibility of pregnancy, it greatly reduces the risk of breast cancer in bitches and prostate cancer in male dogs, and eliminates the risk of testicular cancer in males and pyometra in females.

Your veterinarian should provide your puppy with a thorough dental evaluation at six months of age, ascertaining whether all of the permanent teeth have erupted properly. A home dental-care regimen should be initiated at six months, including brushing weekly and providing good dental devices (such as hard plastic or nylon bones). Regular dental care promotes healthy teeth, fresh breath and a longer life.

DOGS OLDER THAN ONE YEAR

Continue to visit the veterinarian at least once a year. There is no such disease as "old age," but bodily functions do change with age. The eyes and ears are no longer as efficient. Liver, kidney and intestinal functions often decline. Proper dietary changes, recommended by your veterinarian, can make life more pleasant for your aging Eskie and you.

SKIN PROBLEMS

Veterinarians are consulted by dog owners for skin problems more than for any other group of diseases or maladies. A dog's skin is as sensitive, if not more so, than human skin, and both suffer from almost the same ailments (though the occurrence of acne in most breeds is rare). For this reason, veterinary dermatology has developed into a specialty practiced by many veterinarians.

Since many skin problems have visual symptoms that are almost identical, it requires the skill of an experienced veterinary dermatologist to identify and cure many of the more severe skin disorders. Pet shops sell many treatments for skin problems, but most of the treatments are directed at symptoms and not at the underlying problem(s). If your dog is suffering from a skin disorder, you should seek professional assistance as quickly as possible. As with all diseases, the earlier a problem is identified and treated, the more successful can be the cure.

HEREDITARY SKIN DISORDERS

Veterinary dermatologists are currently researching a number of skin disorders that are believed to have hereditary bases. These inherited diseases are transmitted by both parents, who appear (phenotypically) normal but have a recessive gene for the disease, meaning that they carry, but are not affected by, the disease. These diseases pose serious problems to breeders because in some instances there are no methods of identifying carriers. Often the secondary diseases associated with these skin conditions are even more debilitating than the skin disorders themselves, including cancers and respiratory problems.

A SKUNKY PROBLEM

Have you noticed your dog dragging his rump along the floor? If so, it is likely that his anal sacs are impacted or possibly infected. The anal sacs are small pouches located on both sides of the anus under the skin and muscles. They are about the size and shape of a grape and contain a foul-smelling liquid. Their contents are usually emptied when the dog has a bowel movement but, if not emptied completely, they will impact, which will cause your dog much pain. Fortunately, your veterinarian can tend to this problem easily by draining the sacs for the dog. Be aware that your dog might also empty his anal sacs in cases of extreme fright.

Among the hereditary skin disorders, for which the mode of inheritance is known, are acrodermatitis, cutaneous asthenia (Ehlers-Danlos syndrome), sebaceous adenitis, cyclic hematopoiesis, dermatomyositis, IgA deficiency, color dilution alopecia and nodular dermatofibrosis. Some of these disorders are limited to one or two breeds, while others affect a large number of breeds. All inherited diseases must be diagnosed and treated by a veterinary specialist.

PARASITE BITES

Many of us are allergic to insect bites. The bites itch, erupt and may even become infected. Dogs have the same reaction to fleas, ticks and/or mites. When an insect lands on you, you have the chance to whisk it away with your hand. Unfortunately, when a dog is bitten by a flea, tick or mite, he can only scratch it away or bite it. By the time the dog has been bitten, the parasite has done some of its damage. It may also have laid eggs, which will cause further problems in the near future. The itching from parasite bites is probably due to the saliva injected into the site when the parasite sucks the dog's blood

AIRBORNE ALLERGIES

Just as humans suffer from hay fever during the pollinating season, many dogs suffer from the same allergies. When the pollen count is high, your dog might suffer, but don't expect him to sneeze and have a runny nose as a human would. Dogs react to pollen allergies in the same way they react to fleas—they scratch and bite themselves. Dogs, like humans, can be tested for allergens. Discuss the testing with your veterinarian.

AUTO-IMMUNE ILLNESSES

An auto-immune illness is one in which the immune system overacts and does not recognize parts of the affected person; rather, the immune system starts to react as if these parts were foreign and need to be destroyed. An example is rheumatoid arthritis, which occurs when the body does not recognize the joints, thus leading to a very painful and damaging reaction in the joints. This has nothing to do with age, so can occur in children and young dogs. The wear-and-tear arthritis of the older person or dog is osteoarthritis.

Lupus is an auto-immune disease that affects dogs as well as people. It can take variable forms, affecting the kidneys, bones and the skin. It can be fatal, so is treated with steroids, which can themselves have very significant side effects. The steroids calm down the allergic reaction to the body's tissues, which helps the lupus, but the steroids also lessen the body's reaction to real foreign substances such as bacteria as well as thin the skin and bone.

FOOD PROBLEMS

FOOD ALLERGIES

Some dogs can be allergic to many foods that are best-sellers and highly recommended by breeders and veterinarians. Changing the brand of food that you buy may not eliminate the problem if the element to which the dog is allergic is contained in the new brand.

Recognizing a food allergy in a dog can be difficult. Humans often have rashes when we eat foods to which we are allergic, or have swelling of the lips or eyes. Dogs do not usually develop rashes, but react in the same way as they do to an airborne or bite allergy—they itch, scratch and bite. While pollen allergies are usually seasonal, food allergies are year-round problems.

TREATING FOOD ALLERGY

Diagnosis of food allergy is based on a two- to four-week dietary trial with a home-cooked diet fed to the exclusion of all other foods. The diet should consist of boiled rice or potato with a source of protein that the dog has never eaten before, such as fresh or frozen fish, lamb or even something as exotic as pheasant. Water has to be the only drink, and it is really important that no other foods are fed during this trial. If the dog's condition improves, you will need to try the original diet once again to see if the itching resumes. If it does, then this confirms the diagnosis that the dog is allergic to his original diet. The treatment is long-term feeding of something that does not distress the dog's skin, which may be in the form of one of the commercially available hypoallergenic diets or the home-made diet that you created for the allergy trial.

FOOD INTOLERANCE

Food intolerance is the inability of the dog to completely digest certain foods. This occurs because the dog does not have the chemicals necessary to digest some foodstuffs. These chemicals are called enzymes. All puppies have the enzymes necessary to digest canine milk, but some dogs do not have the enzymes to digest a very different form of milk that is commonly found in human households—milk from cows. In such dogs, drinking cows' milk results in loose bowels, stomach pains and the passage of gas.

Dogs often do not have the enzymes to digest soya or other beans. The treatment is to exclude the foodstuffs that upset your Eskie's digestion.

Number-One Killer Disease in Dogs: CANCER

In every age, there is a word associated with a disease or plague that causes humans to shudder. In the 21st century, that word is "cancer." Just as cancer is the leading cause of death in humans, it claims nearly half the lives of dogs that die from a natural disease as well as half the dogs that die over the age of ten years.

Described as a genetic disease, cancer becomes a greater risk as the dog ages. Vets and dog owners have become increasingly aware of the threat of cancer to dogs. Statistics reveal that one dog in every five will develop cancer, the most common of which is skin cancer. Many cancers, including prostate, ovarian and breast cancer, can be avoided by spaying and neutering our dogs by the age of six months.

Early detection of cancer can save or extend a dog's life, so it is absolutely vital for owners to have their dogs examined by a qualified vet or oncologist immediately upon detection of any abnormality. Certain dietary guidelines have also proven to reduce the onset and spread of cancer. Foods based on fish rather than beef, due to the presence of Omega-3 fatty acids, are recommended. Other amino acids such as glutamine have significant benefits for canines, particularly those breeds that show a greater susceptibility to cancer.

Cancer management and treatments promise hope for future generations of canines. Since the disease is genetic, breeders should never breed a dog whose parents, grandparents and any related siblings have developed cancer. It is difficult to know whether to exclude an otherwise healthy dog from a breeding program, as the disease does not manifest itself until the dog's senior years.

RECOGNIZE CANCER WARNING SIGNS

Since early detection can possibly rescue your dog from becoming a cancer statistic, it is essential for owners to recognize the possible signs and seek the assistance of a qualified professional.

- Abnormal bumps or lumps that continue to grow
- Bleeding or discharge from any body cavity
- Persistent stiffness or lameness
- Recurrent sores or sores that do not heal
- Inappetence
- Breathing difficulties
- Weight loss
- Bad breath or odors
- General malaise and fatigue
- Eating and swallowing problems
- Difficulty urinating and defecating

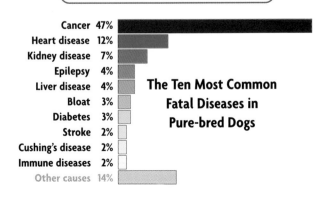

Cancer	47%
Heart disease	12%
Kidney disease	7%
Epilepsy	4%
Liver disease	4%
Bloat	3%
Diabetes	3%
Stroke	2%
Cushing's disease	2%
Immune diseases	2%
Other causes	14%

The Ten Most Common Fatal Diseases in Pure-bred Dogs

A male dog flea, *Ctenocephalides canis.*

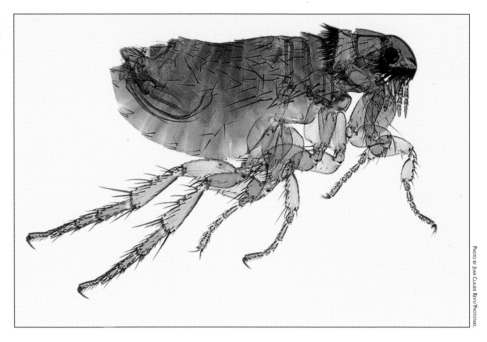

PHOTO BY JEAN CLAUDE REVY/PHOTOTAKE.

EXTERNAL PARASITES

FLEAS

Of all the problems to which dogs are prone, none is more well known and frustrating than fleas. Flea infestation is relatively simple to cure but difficult to prevent. Parasites that are harbored inside the body are a bit more difficult to eradicate but they are easier to control.

To control flea infestation, you have to understand the flea's life cycle. Fleas are often thought of as a summertime problem, but centrally heated homes have changed the patterns and fleas can be found at any time of the year. The most effective method of flea control is a two-stage approach: one stage to kill the adult fleas, and the other to control the development of pre-adult fleas. Unfortunately, no single active ingredient is effective against all stages of the life cycle.

FLEA KILLER CAUTION— "POISON"

Flea-killers are poisonous. You should not spray these toxic chemicals on areas of a dog's body that he licks, including his genitals and his face. Flea killers taken internally are a better answer, but check with your vet in case internal therapy is not advised for your dog.

LIFE CYCLE STAGES

During its life, a flea will pass through four life stages: egg, larva, pupa or nymph and adult. The adult stage is the most visible and irritating stage of the flea life cycle, and this is why the majority of flea-control products concentrate on this stage. The fact is that adult fleas account for only 1% of the total flea population, and the other 99% exist in pre-adult stages, i.e., eggs, larvae and nymphs. The pre-adult stages are barely visible to the naked eye.

THE LIFE CYCLE OF THE FLEA

Eggs are laid on the dog, usually in quantities of about 20 or 30, several times a day. The adult female flea must have a blood meal before each egg-laying session. When first laid, the eggs will cling to the dog's hair, as the eggs are still moist. However, they will quickly dry out and fall from the dog, especially if the dog moves around or scratches. Many eggs will fall off in the dog's favorite area or an area in which he spends a lot of time, such as his bed.

Once the eggs fall from the dog onto the carpet or furniture, they will hatch into larvae. This takes from one to ten days. Larvae are not particularly mobile and will usually travel only a few inches from where they hatch. However, they do have a tendency to move away from bright light and heavy

EN GARDE:
CATCHING FLEAS OFF GUARD!
Consider the following ways to arm yourself against fleas:

- Add a small amount of pennyroyal or eucalyptus oil to your dog's bath. These natural remedies repel fleas.
- Supplement your dog's food with fresh garlic (minced or grated) and a hearty amount of brewer's yeast, both of which ward off fleas.
- Use a flea comb on your dog daily. Submerge fleas in a cup of bleach to kill them quickly.
- Confine the dog to only a few rooms to limit the spread of fleas in the home.
- Vacuum daily...and get all of the crevices! Dispose of the bag every few days until the problem is under control.
- Wash your dog's bedding daily. Cover cushions where your dog sleeps with towels, and wash the towels often.

traffic—under furniture and behind doors are common places to find high quantities of flea larvae.

The flea larvae feed on dead organic matter, including adult flea feces, until they are ready to change into adult fleas. Fleas will usually remain as larvae for around seven days. After this period, the larvae will pupate into protective pupae. While inside the pupae, the larvae will undergo metamorphosis and change into

Fleas have been measured as being able to jump 300,000 times and can jump over 150 times their length in any direction, including straight up.

adult fleas. This can take as little time as a few days, but the adult fleas can remain inside the pupae waiting to hatch for up to two years. The pupae are signaled to hatch by certain stimuli, such as physical pressure—the pupae's being stepped on, heat from an animal's lying on the pupae or increased carbon-dioxide levels and vibrations—indicating that a suitable host is available.

Once hatched, the adult flea must feed within a few days. Once the adult flea finds a host, it will not leave voluntarily. It only becomes dislodged by grooming or the host animal's scratching. The adult flea will remain on the

host for the duration of its life unless forcibly removed.

TREATING THE ENVIRONMENT AND THE DOG

Treating fleas should be a two-pronged attack. First, the environment needs to be treated; this includes carpets and furniture, especially the dog's bedding and areas underneath furniture. The environment should be treated with a household spray containing an Insect Growth Regulator (IGR) and an insecticide to kill the adult fleas. Most IGRs are effective against eggs and larvae; they actually mimic the fleas' own hormones and stop the eggs and larvae from developing into adult fleas. There are currently no treatments available to attack the pupa stage of the life cycle, so the adult insecticide is used to kill the newly hatched adult fleas before they find a host. Most IGRs are active for many months, while adult insecticides are only active

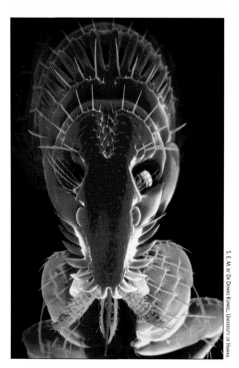

A scanning electron micrograph of a dog or cat flea, *Ctenocephalides*, magnified more than 100x. This image has been colorized for effect.

THE LIFE CYCLE OF THE FLEA

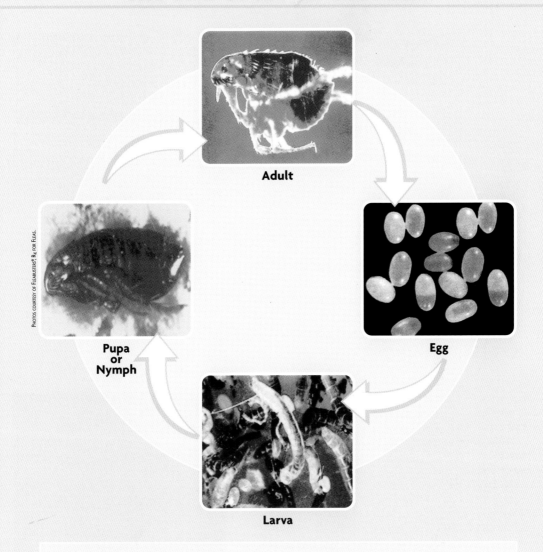

Adult

Egg

Larva

Pupa or Nymph

Fleas have been around for millions of years and have adapted to changing host animals. They are able to go through a complete life cycle in less than one month or they can extend their lives to almost two years by remaining as pupae or cocoons. They do not need blood or any other food for up to 20 months.

INSECT GROWTH REGULATOR (IGR)

Two types of products should be used when treating fleas—a product to treat the pet and a product to treat the home. Adult fleas represent less than 1% of the flea population. The pre-adult fleas (eggs, larvae and pupae) represent more than 99% of the flea population and are found in the environment; it is in the case of pre-adult fleas that products containing an Insect Growth Regulator (IGR) should be used in the home.

IGRs are a new class of compounds used to prevent the development of insects. They do not kill the insect outright, but instead use the insect's biology against it to stop it from completing its growth. Products that contain methoprene are the world's first and leading IGRs. Used to control fleas and other insects, this type of IGR will stop flea larvae from developing and protect the house for up to seven months.

The American dog tick, *Dermacentor variabilis*, is probably the most common tick found on dogs. Look at the strength in its eight legs! No wonder it's hard to detach them.

is to apply an adult insecticide to the dog. Traditionally, this would be in the form of a collar or a spray, but more recent innovations include digestible insecticides that poison the fleas when they ingest the dog's blood. Alternatively, there are drops that, when placed on the back of the dog's neck, spread throughout the hair and skin to kill adult fleas.

TICKS

Though not as common as fleas, ticks are found all over the tropical and temperate world. They don't bite, like fleas; they harpoon. They dig their sharp proboscis (nose) into the dog's skin and drink the blood. Their only food and drink is dog's

for a few days.

When treating with a household spray, it is a good idea to vacuum before applying the product. This stimulates as many pupae as possible to hatch into adult fleas. The vacuum cleaner should also be treated with an insecticide to prevent the eggs and larvae that have been collected in the vacuum bag from hatching.

The second stage of treatment

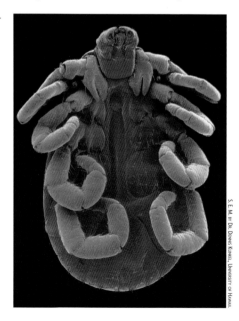

S. E. M. BY DR. DENNIS KUNKEL, UNIVERSITY OF HAWAII.

blood. Dogs can get Lyme disease, Rocky Mountain spotted fever, tick bite paralysis and many other diseases from ticks. They may live where fleas are found and they like to hide in cracks or seams in walls. They are controlled the same way fleas are controlled.

The American dog tick, *Dermacentor variabilis*, may well be the most common dog tick in many geographical areas, especially those areas where the climate is hot and humid. Most dog ticks have life expectancies of a week to six months, depending upon climatic conditions. They can neither jump nor fly, but they can crawl slowly and can range up to 16 feet to reach a sleeping or unsuspecting dog.

MITES

Just as fleas and ticks can be problematic for your dog, mites can also lead to an itchy nuisance. Microscopic in size, mites are related to ticks and generally take up permanent residence on their host animal—in this case, your dog! The term *mange* refers to any infestation caused by one of the mighty mites, of which there are six varieties that concern dog owners.

Demodex mites cause a condition known as demodicosis (sometimes called red mange or

DEER-TICK CROSSING

The great outdoors may be fun for your dog, but it also is a home to dangerous ticks. Deer ticks carry a bacterium known as *Borrelia burgdorferi* and are most active in the autumn and spring. When infections are caught early, penicillin and tetracycline are effective antibiotics, but, if left untreated, the bacteria may cause neurological, kidney and cardiac problems as well as long-term trouble with walking and painful joints.

The head of an American dog tick, *Dermacentor variabilis*, enlarged and colorized for effect.

The mange mite, *Psoroptes bovis*, can infest cattle and other domestic animals.

PHOTO BY JAMES HAYDEN/YOAV/PHOTOTAKE

follicular mange), in which the mites live in the dog's hair follicles and sebaceous glands in larger-than-normal numbers. This type of mange is commonly passed from the dam to her puppies and usually shows up on the puppies' muzzles, though demodicosis is not transferable from one normal dog to another. Most dogs recover from this type of mange without any treatment, though topical therapies are commonly prescribed by the vet.

Human lice look like dog lice; the two are closely related.
PHOTO BY DWIGHT R. KUHN.

The *Cheyletiellosis* mite is the hook-mouthed culprit associated with "walking dandruff," a condition that affects dogs as well as cats and rabbits. This mite lives on the surface of the animal's skin and is readily transferable through direct or indirect contact with an affected animal. The dandruff is present in the form of scaly skin, which may or may not be itchy. If not treated, this mange can affect a whole kennel of dogs and can be spread to humans as well.

The *Sarcoptes* mite causes intense itching on the dog in the form of a condition known as scabies or sarcoptic mange. The cycle of the *Sarcoptes* mite lasts about three weeks, and the mites live in the top layer of the dog's skin (epidermis), preferably in areas with little hair. Scabies is highly contagious and can be passed to humans. Sometimes an allergic reaction to the mite worsens the severe itching associated with sarcoptic mange.

Ear mites, *Otodectes cynotis,* lead to otodectic mange, which most commonly affects the outer ear canal of the dog, though other areas can be affected as well. Dogs with ear-mite infestation commonly scratch at their ears, causing further irritation, and shake their heads. Dark brown droppings in the outer ear confirm the diagnosis. Your vet can prescribe a treatment to flush out the ears and kill any eggs in the ears. A complete month of treatment is necessary to cure the mange.

Two other mites, less common in dogs, include *Dermanyssus gallinae* (the poultry or red mite) and *Eutrombicula alfreddugesi* (the North American mite associated with trombiculidiasis or chigger infestation). The poultry mite frequently lives on chickens, but can transfer to dogs who spend time near farm animals. Chigger infestation affects dogs in the

NOT A DROP TO DRINK
Never allow your dog to swim in polluted water or public areas where water quality can be suspect. Even perfectly clear water can harbor parasites, many of which can cause serious to fatal illnesses in canines. Areas inhabited by water-fowl and other wildlife are especially dangerous.

Central US who have exposure to woodlands. The types of mange caused by both of these mites are treatable by vets.

INTERNAL PARASITES

Most animals—fishes, birds and mammals, including dogs and humans—have worms and other parasites that live inside their bodies. According to Dr. Herbert R. Axelrod, the fish pathologist, there are two kinds of parasites: dumb and smart. The smart parasites live in peaceful cooperation with their hosts (symbiosis), while the dumb parasites kill their hosts. Most worm infections are relatively easy to control. If they are not controlled, they weaken the host dog to the point that other medical problems occur, but they do not kill the host as dumb parasites would.

A brown dog tick, *Rhipicephalus sanguineus*, is an uncommon but annoying tick found on dogs.

PHOTO BY CAROLINA BIOLOGICAL SUPPLY/PHOTOTAKE.

DO NOT MIX
Never mix parasite-control products without first consulting your vet. Some products can become toxic when combined with others and can cause fatal consequences.

Photo by Carolina Biological Supply/Phototake

The roundworm *Rhabditis* can infect both dogs and humans.

The roundworm, *Ascaris lumbricoides.*

ROUNDWORMS

Average-size dogs can pass 1,360,000 roundworm eggs every day. For example, if there were only 1 million dogs in the world, the world would be saturated with thousands of tons of dog feces. These feces would contain around 15,000,000,000 roundworm eggs.

Up to 31% of home yards and children's sand boxes in the US contain roundworm eggs.

Flushing dog's feces down the toilet is not a safe practice because the usual sewage treatments do not destroy roundworm eggs.

Infected puppies start shedding roundworm eggs at three weeks of age. They can be infected by their mother's milk.

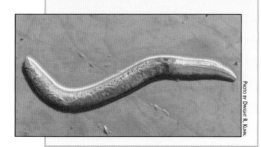

Photo by Dwight R. Kuhn

ROUNDWORMS

The roundworms that infect dogs are known scientifically as *Toxocara canis*. They live in the dog's intestines and shed eggs continually. It has been estimated that a dog produces about 6 or more ounces of feces every day. Each ounce of feces averages hundreds of thousands of roundworm eggs. There are no known areas in which dogs roam that do not contain roundworm eggs. The greatest danger of roundworms is that they infect people, too! It is wise to have your dog tested regularly for roundworms.

In young puppies, roundworms cause bloated bellies, diarrhea, coughing and vomiting, and are transmitted from the dam (through blood or milk). Affected puppies will not appear as animated as normal puppies. The worms appear spaghetti-like, measuring as long as 6 inches. Adult dogs can acquire roundworms through coprophagia (eating contaminated feces) or by killing rodents that carry roundworms.

Roundworm infection can kill puppies and cause severe problems in adults, as the hatched larvae travel to the lungs and trachea through the bloodstream. Cleanliness is the best preventative for roundworms. Always pick up after your dog and dispose of feces in appropriate receptacles.

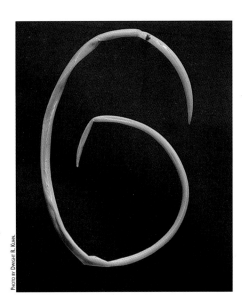

PHOTO BY DWIGHT R. KUHN.

HOOKWORMS

In the United States, dog owners have to be concerned about four different species of hookworm, the most common and most serious of which is *Ancylostoma caninum,* which prefers warm climates. The others are *Ancylostoma braziliense, Ancylostoma tubaeforme* and *Uncinaria stenocephala,* the latter of which is a concern to dogs living in the Northern US and Canada, as this species prefers cold climates. Hookworms are dangerous to humans as well as to dogs and cats, and can be the cause of severe anemia due to iron deficiency. The worm uses its teeth to attach itself to the dog's intestines and changes the site of its attachment about six times per day. Each time the worm

repositions itself, the dog loses blood and can become anemic. *Ancylostoma caninum* is the most likely of the four species to cause anemia in the dog.

Symptoms of hookworm infection include dark stools, weight loss, general weakness, pale coloration and anemia, as well as possible skin problems. Fortunately, hookworms are easily purged from the affected dog with a number of medications that have proven effective. Discuss these with your vet. Most heartworm preventatives include a hookworm insecticide as well.

Owners also must be aware that hookworms can infect humans, who can acquire the larvae through exposure to contaminated feces. Since the worms cannot complete their life cycle on a human, the worms simply infest the skin and cause irritation. This condition is known as cutaneous larva migrans syndrome. As a preventative, use disposable gloves or a "poop-scoop" to pick up your dog's droppings and prevent your dog (or neighborhood cats) from defecating in children's play areas.

The hookworm, *Ancylostoma caninum.*

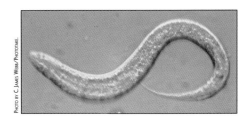

PHOTO BY C. JAMES WEBB/PHOTOTAKE.

The infective stage of the hookworm larva.

TAPEWORMS

Humans, rats, squirrels, foxes, coyotes, wolves and domestic dogs are all susceptible to tapeworm infection. Except in humans, tapeworms are usually not a fatal infection. Infected individuals can harbor 1000 parasitic worms.

Tapeworms, like some other types of worm, are hermaphroditic, meaning male and female in the same worm.

If dogs eat infected rats or mice, or anything else infected with tapeworm, they get the tapeworm disease. One month after attaching to a dog's intestine, the worm starts shedding eggs. These eggs are infective immediately. Infective eggs can live for a few months without a host animal.

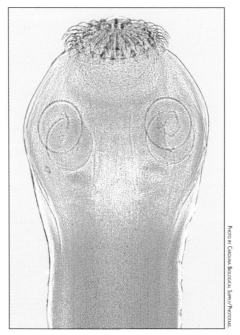

The head and rostellum (the round prominence on the scolex) of a tapeworm, which infects dogs and humans.

PHOTO BY CAROLINA BIOLOGICAL SUPPLY/PHOTOTAKE.

TAPEWORMS

There are many species of tapeworm, all of which are carried by fleas! The most common tapeworm affecting dogs is known as *Dipylidium caninum*. The dog eats the flea and starts the tapeworm cycle. Humans can also be infected with tapeworms—so don't eat fleas! Fleas are so small that your dog could pass them onto your hands, your plate or your food and thus make it possible for you to ingest a flea that is carrying tapeworm eggs.

While tapeworm infection is not life-threatening in dogs (smart parasite!), it can be the cause of a very serious liver disease for humans. About 50% of the humans infected with *Echinococcus multilocularis*, a type of tapeworm that causes alveolar hydatid, perish.

WHIPWORMS

In North America, whipworms are counted among the most common parasitic worms in dogs. The whipworm's scientific name is *Trichuris vulpis*. These worms attach themselves in the lower parts of the intestine, where they feed. Affected dogs may only experience upset tummies, colic and diarrhea. These worms, however, can live for months or years in the dog, beginning their larval stage in the small intestine, spending their adult stage in the large intestine and finally passing infective eggs through the dog's feet. The only way to detect whipworms is through a fecal examination, though this is not always foolproof. Treatment for whipworms is tricky, due to the worms' unusual life-cycle pattern, and very often dogs are reinfected due to exposure to infective eggs on the ground. The whipworm eggs can survive in the environment for as long as five years; thus, cleaning up droppings in your own backyard as well as in public places is absolutely essential for sanitation purposes and the health of your dog and others.

THREADWORMS
Though less common than round-worms, hookworms and those previously mentioned, thread-

worms concern dog owners in the Southwestern US and Gulf Coast area where the climate is hot and humid. Living in the small intes-tine of the dog, this worm meas-ures a mere 2 millimeters and is round in shape. Like that of the whipworm, the threadworm's life cycle is very complex and the eggs and larvae are passed through the feces. A deadly disease in humans, *Strongyloides* readily infects people, and the handling of feces is the most common means of trans-mission. Threadworms are most often seen in young puppies; bloody diarrhea and pneumonia are symptoms. Sick puppies must be isolated and treated immedi-ately; vets recommend a follow-up treatment one month later.

HEARTWORM PREVENTATIVES

There are many heartworm preventatives on the market, many of which are sold at your veterinarian's office. These products can be given daily or monthly, depending on the manufacturer's instructions. All of these preventatives contain chemical insecticides directed at killing heartworms, which leads to some controversy among dog owners. In effect, heartworm preventatives are neces-sary evils, though you should determine how necessary based on your pet's lifestyle. There is no doubt that heartworm is a dreadful disease that threatens the lives of dogs. However, the likelihood of your dog's being bitten by an infected mosquito is slim in most places, and a mosquito-repellent (or an herbal remedy such as Wormwood or

Black Walnut) is much safer for your dog and will not compromise his immune system (the way heartworm preventatives will). Should you decide to use the tradi-tional preventative "medications," you can consider giving the pill every other or third month. Since the toxins in the pill will kill the heartworms at all stages of develop-ment, the pill would be effective in killing larvae, nymphs or adults, and it takes four months for the larvae to reach the adult stage. Thus, there is no rationale to poison-ing the dog's system on a monthly basis. Lastly, do not give the pill during the winter months, since there are no mosquitoes around to pass on their infection, unless you live in a tropical environment.

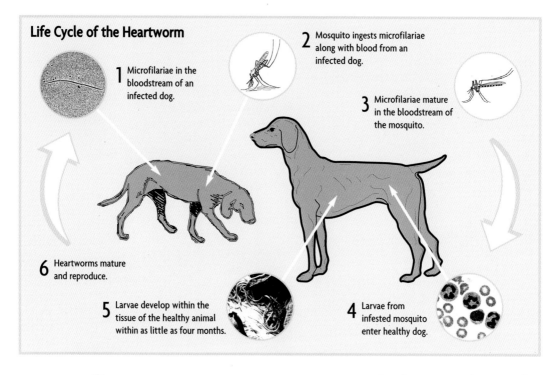

Life Cycle of the Heartworm

1 Microfilariae in the bloodstream of an infected dog.

2 Mosquito ingests microfilariae along with blood from an infected dog.

3 Microfilariae mature in the bloodstream of the mosquito.

6 Heartworms mature and reproduce.

5 Larvae develop within the tissue of the healthy animal within as little as four months.

4 Larvae from infested mosquito enter healthy dog.

HEARTWORMS

Heartworms are thin, extended worms up to 12 inches long, which live in a dog's heart and the major blood vessels surrounding it. Dogs may have up to 200 worms. Symptoms may be loss of energy, loss of appetite, coughing, the development of a pot belly and anemia.

Heartworms are transmitted by mosquitoes. The mosquito drinks the blood of an infected dog and takes in larvae with the blood. The larvae, called microfilariae, develop within the body of the mosquito and are passed on to the next dog bitten after the larvae mature. It takes two to three weeks for the larvae to develop to the infective stage within the body of the mosquito. Dogs are usually treated at about six weeks of age and maintained on a prophylactic dose given monthly.

Blood testing for heartworms is not necessarily indicative of how seriously your dog is infected. Although this is a dangerous disease, it is not easy for a dog to be infected. Discuss the various preventatives with your vet, as there are many different types now available. Together you can decide on a safe course of prevention for your dog.

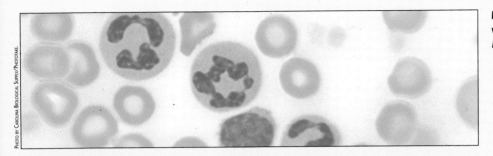

Magnified heart-worm larvae, *Dirofilaria immitis*.

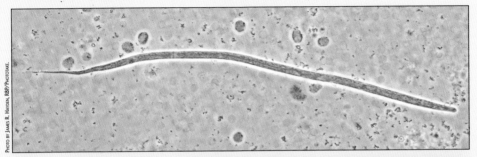

Heartworm, *Dirofilaria immitis*.

The heart of a dog infected with canine heart-worm, *Dirofilaria immitis*.

HOMEOPATHY:
an alternative to conventional medicine

"Less is Most"

Using this principle, the strength of a homeopathic remedy is measured by the number of serial dilutions that were undertaken to create it. The greater the number of serial dilutions, the greater the strength of the homeopathic remedy. The potency of a remedy that has been made by making a dilution of 1 part in 100 parts (or 1/100) is 1c or 1cH. If this remedy is subjected to a series of further dilutions, each one being 1/100, a more dilute and stronger remedy is produced. If the remedy is diluted in this way six times, it is called 6c or 6cH. A dilution of 6c is 1 part in 1,000,000,000,000. In general, higher potencies in more frequent doses are better for acute symptoms and lower potencies in more infrequent doses are more useful for chronic, long-standing problems.

CURING OUR DOGS NATURALLY

Holistic medicine means treating the whole animal as a unique, perfect, living being. Generally, holistic treatments do not suppress the symptoms that the body naturally produces, as do most medications prescribed by conventional doctors and vets. Holistic methods seek to cure disease by regaining balance and harmony in the patient's environment. Some of these methods include use of nutritional therapy, herbs, flower essences, aromatherapy, acupuncture, massage, chiropractic and, of course, the most popular holistic approach, homeopathy.

Homeopathy is a theory or system of treating illness with small doses of substances which, if administered in larger quantities, would produce the symptoms that the patient already has. This approach is often described as "like cures like." Although modern veterinary medicine is geared toward the "quick fix," homeopathy relies on the belief that, given the time, the body is able to heal itself and return to its natural, healthy state.

Choosing a remedy to cure a problem in our dogs is the difficult part of homeopathy. Consult with your vet for a professional diagnosis of your dog's symptoms. Often

these symptoms require immediate conventional care. If your vet is willing and knowledgeable, you may attempt a homeopathic remedy. Be aware that cortisone prevents homeopathic remedies from working. There are hundreds of possibilities and combinations to cure many problems in dogs, from basic physical problems such as excessive shedding, fleas or other parasites, unattractive doggy odor, bad breath, upset tummy, obesity, dry, oily or dull coat, diarrhea, ear problems or eye discharge (including tears and dry or mucousy matter), to behavioral abnormalities such as fear of loud noises, habitual licking, poor appetite, excessive barking and various phobias. From alumina to zincum metallicum, the remedies span the planet and the imagination…from flowers and weeds to chemicals, insect droppings, diesel smoke and volcanic ash.

Using "Like to Treat Like"

Unlike conventional medicines that suppress symptoms, homeopathic remedies treat illnesses with small doses of substances that, if administered in larger quantities, would produce the symptoms that the patient already has. While the same homeopathic remedy can be used to treat different symptoms in different dogs, here are some interesting remedies and their uses.

Apis Mellifica
(made from honey bee venom) can be used for allergies or to reduce swelling that occurs in acutely infected kidneys.

Diesel Smoke
can be used to help control travel sickness.

Calcarea Fluorica
(made from calcium fluoride, which helps harden bone structure) can be useful in treating hard lumps in tissues.

Natrum Muriaticum
(made from common salt, sodium chloride) is useful in treating thin, thirsty dogs.

Nitricum Acidum
(made from nitric acid) is used for symptoms you would expect to see from contact with acids, such as lesions, especially where the skin joins the linings of body orifices or openings such as the lips and nostrils.

Symphytum
(made from the herb Knitbone, *Symphytum officianale*) is used to encourage bones to heal.

Urtica Urens
(made from the common stinging nettle) is used in treating painful, irritating rashes.

SHOWING YOUR

AMERICAN ESKIMO DOG

When you purchase your American Eskimo Dog, you will make it clear to the breeder whether you want one just as a lovable companion and pet, or if you hope to be buying an Eskie with show prospects. No reputable breeder will sell you a young puppy and tell you that it is *definitely* of show quality, for so much can go wrong during the early months of a puppy's development. If you plan to show, what you ideally will have acquired is a puppy with "show potential."

To the novice, exhibiting an American Eskimo in the show ring may look easy, but it takes a lot of hard work and devotion to do top winning at a show such as the prestigious Westminster Kennel Club dog show, not to mention a little luck too!

The first concept that the canine novice learns when watching a dog show is that each dog first competes against members of his own breed. Once the judge has selected the best member of each breed (Best of Breed), provided that the show is judged on a Group system, that chosen dog will compete with other dogs in his group. Finally, the dogs chosen first in each group will compete for Best in Show.

The second concept that you must understand is that the dogs are not actually compared against one another. The judge compares each dog against his breed standard, the written description of the ideal specimen that is approved by the hosting kennel club. While some early breed standards were indeed based on specific dogs that were famous or popular, many dedicated enthusiasts say that a perfect specimen, to the woe of dog breeders around the globe, does not exist. Breeders attempt to get as close to this ideal as possible with every litter, but theoretically the "perfect" dog is so elusive that it is impossible.

Shows for Eskies are sponsored by the American Kennel

AKC GROUPS

For showing purposes, the American Kennel Club divides its recognized breeds into seven groups: Non-Sporting Dogs (of which the Eskie is a member), Sporting Dogs, Hounds, Working Dogs, Terriers, Toys, and Herding Dogs.

Club (AKC) and the United Kennel Club (UKC), the latter club having promoted the breed for decades. If you are interested in exploring the world of dog showing, your best bet is to join your local breed club or the national club, which is the American Eskimo Dog Club of America for AKC-registered dogs, and the National American Eskimo Dog Association for UKC-registered dogs. These clubs host both regional and national specialties, shows only for American Eskimos, which can include conformation as well as obedience and agility trials. Even if you have no intention of competing with your Eskie, a specialty is like a festival for lovers of the breed, who congregate to share their favorite topic: American Eskimo Dogs! Clubs also send out newsletters, and some organize training days and seminars in order that people may learn more about their chosen breed.

To locate the breed club closest to you, contact the kennel club, with which your Eskie is registered. These kennel clubs furnish the rules and regulations for all of these events plus general dog registration and other basic requirements of dog ownership. This chapter discusses shows as organized by the AKC.

The American Kennel Club offers three kinds of conformation shows: an all-breed show (for all AKC-recognized breeds); a specialty show (for one breed only,

The outgoing Eskie, with his beguiling expression and striking white coat, is a spectacular sight in the show ring.

usually sponsored by the parent club); and a Group show (for all breeds in the group). For a dog to become an AKC champion of record, the dog must accumulate 15 points at the shows from at least three different judges, including two "majors." A "major" is defined as a three-, four- or five-point win, and the number of points per win is determined by the number of dogs entered in the show on that day. Depending on the breed, the number of points that are awarded varies. In numerically strong breeds, more dogs are needed to rack up the points, while less dogs are needed in breeds with fewer numbers.

At any dog show, only one dog and one bitch of each breed can

CLUB CONTACTS

You can get information about dog shows from the national kennel clubs:

American Kennel Club
5580 Centerview Dr., Raleigh, NC 27606-3390
www.akc.org

United Kennel Club
100 E. Kilgore Road, Kalamazoo, MI 49002
www.ukcdogs.com

Canadian Kennel Club
89 Skyway Ave., Suite 100, Etobicoke, Ontario
M9W 6R4, Canada
www.ckc.ca

win points. Dog showing does not offer "co-ed" classes. Dogs and bitches never compete against each other in the classes. Non-champion dogs are called "class dogs" because they compete in one of five classes. Dogs are entered in a particular class depending on age and previous show wins. To begin, there is the Puppy Class (for 6- to 9-month-olds and for 9- to 12-month-olds); this class is followed by the Novice Class (for dogs that have not won any first prizes except in the Puppy Class or three first prizes in the Novice Class and have not accumulated any points toward their champion title), the Bred-by-Exhibitor Class (for dogs handled by their breeders or by one of the breeder's immediate family), the American-bred Class (for dogs bred in the US) and the Open Class (for any dog that is not a champion).

The judge at the show begins judging the Puppy Class, first dogs and then bitches, and proceeds through the classes. The judge places his winners first through fourth in each class. In the Winners Class, the first-place winners of each class compete with one another to determine Winners Dog and Winners Bitch. The judge also places a Reserve Winners Dog and Reserve Winners Bitch, which could be awarded the points in the case of a disqualification. The Winners Dog and Winners Bitch, the two that are awarded the points for the breed, then compete with any champions of record entered in the show. The judge reviews the Winners Dog, Winners Bitch and all of the champions to select his Best of Breed. The Best of Winners is selected between the Winners Dog and Winners Bitch. Were one of these two to be selected Best of Breed, he or she would automatically be named Best of Winners as well. Finally the judge selects his Best of Opposite Sex to the Best of Breed winner.

At a Group show or all-breed show, the Best of Breed winners from each breed then compete against one another for Group One through Group Four. The judge compares each Best of Breed to his respective breed standard, and the dog that most closely lives up to the ideal for his breed is selected as Group One. Finally, all seven group winners (from the Non-Sporting Group, Working Group, Hound Group, etc.) compete for Best in Show.

To find out about AKC shows in your area, you can subscribe to the American Kennel Club's monthly magazine, the *American Kennel Gazette* and the accompanying *Events Calendar*. You can also look in your local newspaper for advertisements for dog shows in your area or go on the Internet to the AKC's website, www.akc.org.

If your Eskie is six months of age or older and registered with the AKC, you can enter him in a dog show where the breed is offered classes. Provided that your Eskie does not have a disqualifying fault, he can compete. Only unaltered dogs can be entered in a dog show, so if you have spayed or neutered your Eskie, he or she cannot compete in conformation shows. The reason for this is simple. Dog shows are the main forum to prove which representatives in a breed are worthy of being bred. Only dogs that have achieved championships—the "seal of approval" for quality in pure-bred dogs—should be bred. Altered dogs, however, can participate in other events such as obedience trials and the AKC's Canine Good Citizen® program.

Before you actually step into the ring, you would be well advised to sit back and observe the judge's ring procedure. If it is your first time in the ring, do not be over-anxious and run to the front of the line. It is much better to stand back and study how the exhibitor in front of you is performing. The judge asks each handler to "stack" the dog, hopefully showing the dog off to his best advantage. The judge will observe the dog from a distance and from different angles, and approach the dog to check his teeth, overall structure, alertness and muscle tone, as well as consider how well the dog "conforms" to the standard. Most importantly, the judge will have the exhibitor move the dog around the ring in some pattern that he should specify. Finally, the judge will give the dog one last look before moving on to the next exhibitor.

If you are not in the top four in your class at your first show, do not be discouraged. Be patient and consistent, and you may eventually find yourself in a winning line-up.

The handler will sometimes help the dog into the correct standing position to show the dog off in the best possible way.

SHOW-RING ETIQUETTE

Just as with anything else, there is a certain etiquette to the show ring that can only be learned through experience. Showing your dog can be quite intimidating to you as a novice when it seems as if everyone else knows what he is doing. You can familiarize yourself with ring procedure beforehand by taking showing classes to prepare you and your dog for conformation showing, and by talking with experienced handlers. When you are in the ring, it is very important to pay attention and listen to the instructions you are given by the judge about where to move your dog. Remember, even the most skilled handlers had to start somewhere. Keep it up and you too will become a proficient handler as you gain practice and experience.

Remember that the winners were once in your shoes and have devoted many hours and much money to earn the placement. If you find that your dog is losing every time and never getting a nod, it may be time to consider a different dog sport or to just enjoy your Eskie as a pet. Parent clubs offer other events, such as agility, tracking, obedience, instinct tests and more, which may be of interest to the owner of a well-trained American Eskimo Dog.

OBEDIENCE TRIALS

Obedience trials in the US trace back to the early 1930s when organized obedience training was developed to demonstrate how well dog and owner could work together. The pioneer of obedience trials is Mrs. Helen Whitehouse Walker, a Standard Poodle fancier, who designed a series of exercises after the Associated Sheep, Police Army Dog Society of Great Britain. Since the days of Mrs. Walker, obedience trials have grown by leaps and bounds, and today there are over 2,000 trials held in the US every year, with more than 100,000 dogs competing. Any registered dog can enter an obedience trial, regardless of conformational disqualifications or neutering.

Obedience trials are divided into three levels of progressive difficulty. At the first level, the Novice, dogs compete for the title Companion Dog (CD); at the intermediate level, the Open, dogs compete for the title Companion Dog Excellent (CDX); and at the advanced level, the Utility, dogs compete for the title Utility Dog (UD). Classes are sub-divided into "A" (for beginners) and "B" (for more experienced handlers). A perfect score at any level is 200, and a dog must score 170 or better to earn a "leg," of which three are needed to earn the title. To earn points, the dog must score more than 50% of the available points in each exercise; the possible points range from 20 to 40.

Once a dog has earned the UD title, he can compete with other proven obedience dogs for the coveted title of Utility Dog Excellent (UDX), which requires that the dog win "legs" in ten shows. Utility Dogs who earn "legs" in Open B and Utility B earn points toward their Obedience Trial Champion title. In 1977, the title Obedience Trial Champion (OTCh.) was established by the AKC. To become an OTCh., a dog needs to earn 100 points, which requires three first places in Open B and Utility under three different judges.

The Grand Prix of obedience trials, the AKC National Obedience Invitational gives qualifying Utility Dogs the chance to win the newest and highest title: National Obedience Champion (NOC). Only the top 25 ranked obedience dogs, plus any dog ranked in the top 3 in his breed, are allowed to compete.

AGILITY TRIALS

Having had its origins in the UK back in 1977, AKC agility had its official beginning in the US in August 1994, when the first licensed agility trials were held. The AKC allows all registered breeds (including Miscellaneous Class breeds) to participate, providing the dog is 12 months of age or older. Agility is designed so that the handler demonstrates how well the dog can work at his side. The handler directs his dog over an obstacle course that includes jumps as well as tires, the dog walk, weave poles, pipe tunnels, collapsed tunnels, etc. While working his way through the course, the dog must keep one eye and ear on the handler and the rest of his body on the course. The handler gives verbal and hand signals to guide the dog through the course.

The first organization to promote agility trials in the US was the United States Dog Agility Association, Inc. (USDAA), which was established in 1986 and spawned numerous member clubs around the country. The USDAA as well as the AKC and UKC offer titles to winning dogs.

Agility is great fun for dog and owner with many rewards for everyone involved. Interested owners should join a training club with obstacles and handlers who can introduce you and your dog to the "ropes" (and tires, tunnels, etc.).

AMERICAN ESKIMO DOG

As an American Eskimo Dog owner, you have selected your dog so that you and your loved ones can have a companion, a protector, a friend and a four-legged family member. You invest time, money and effort to care for and train the family's new charge. Of course, this chosen canine behaves perfectly! Well, perfectly like a *dog*.

THINK LIKE A DOG

Dogs do not think like humans, nor do humans think like dogs, though we try. Unfortunately, a dog is incapable of comprehending how humans think, so the responsibility falls on the owner to adopt a viable canine mindset. Dogs cannot rationalize, and they exist in the present moment. Many a dog owner makes the mistake in training of thinking that he can reprimand his dog for something the dog did a while ago. Basically, you cannot even reprimand a dog for something he did 20 seconds ago! Either catch him in the act or forget it! It is a waste of your and your dog's time—in his mind, you are reprimanding him for whatever he is doing at that moment.

The following behavioral problems represent some which owners most commonly encounter. Every dog is unique and every situation is unique. No author could purport for you to solve your Eskie's problems simply by reading a chapter in a breed book. Here we outline some basic "dogspeak" so that owners' chances of solving behavioral problems are increased. Discuss bad habits with your vet and he can recommend a behavioral specialist to consult in appropriate cases. Since behavioral abnormalities are the main reason that owners abandon their pets, we hope that you will make a valiant effort to solve your Eskie's problems. Patience and understanding are virtues that must dwell in every pet-loving household.

SEPARATION ANXIETY

Recognized by behaviorists as the most common form of stress for dogs, separation anxiety can also lead to destructive behaviors in your dog. It's more than your Eskie's howling his displeasure at your leaving the house and his being left alone. This is a normal reaction, no different than the child who cries as his mother leaves him on the first day at school. Separation anxiety is more serious. In fact, if you are constantly with your dog, he will come to expect you with him all of the time, making it even more traumatic for him when you are not there.

Obviously, you enjoy spending time with your dog, and he thrives on your love and attention. However, it should not become a dependent relationship in which he is heartbroken without you. This broken heart can also lead to destructive behavior as well as loss of appetite, depression and lack of interest in play and inter-action. Canine behaviorists have been spending much time and energy to help owners better understand the significance of this stressful condition.

One thing you can do to mini-

mize separation anxiety is to make your entrances and exits as low-key as possible. Do not give your dog a long drawn-out goodbye, and do not lavish him with hugs and kisses when you return. This is giving in to the attention that he craves, and it will only make him miss it more when you are away. Another thing you can try is to give your dog a treat when you leave; this will not only keep him occupied and keep his mind off the fact that you have left, but it will also help him associate your leaving with a pleasant experi-ence.

You may have to accustom your dog to being left alone in intervals. Of course, when your dog starts whimpering as you approach the door, your first instinct will be to run to him and comfort him, but do not do it! Eventually he will adjust to your absence. His anxiety stems from being placed in an unfamiliar situ-

Alone in the yard is not the way for the Eskie to spend most of his time. He needs to be part of life in the home, doing things with his owner, just as much as he needs periods of exercise outdoors.

"LONELY WOLF"

The number of dogs that suffer from separation anxiety is on the rise as more and more pet owners find them-selves at work all day. New attention is being paid to this problem, which is especially hard to diagnose since it is only evident when the dog is alone. Research is currently being done to help educate dog owners about sepa-ration anxiety and how they can help minimize this problem in their dogs.

ation; by familiarizing him with being alone, he will learn that he will survive. That is not to say you should purposely leave your dog home alone, but the dog needs to know that, while he can depend on you for his care, you do not have to be by his side 24 hours a day. Some behaviorists recommend tiring the dog out before you leave home—take him for a good long walk or engage in a game of fetch in the yard.

When the dog is alone in the house, he should be placed in his crate—another distinct advantage to crate training your dog. The crate should be placed in his happy family area, where he normally sleeps and already feels comfortable, thereby making him feel more at ease when he is alone. Be sure to give the dog a special chew toy to enjoy while he settles into his crate.

AGGRESSION

Although the Eskie is not an aggressive breed by nature, aggression is a problem that concerns all responsible dog owners. Aggression can be a very big problem in dogs, and, when not controlled, always becomes dangerous. An aggressive dog, no matter the size, may lunge at, bite or even attack a person or another dog. Aggressive behavior is not to be tolerated. It is more than just inappropriate behavior; it is painful for a family to watch their dog become unpredictable in his behavior to the point where they are afraid of him. While not all aggressive behavior is dangerous, things like growl-

PHARMACEUTICAL FIX

There are two drugs specifically designed to treat mental problems in dogs. About seven million dogs each year are destroyed because owners can no longer tolerate their dogs' behavior, according to Nicholas Dodman, a specialist in animal behavior at Tufts University in Massachusetts.

The first drug, Clomicalm, is prescribed for dogs suffering from separation anxiety, which is said to cause them to react when left alone by barking, chewing their owners' belongings, drooling copiously or defecating or urinating inside the home.

The second drug, Anipryl, is recommended for cognitive dysfunction syndrome or "old-dog syndrome," a mental deterioration that comes with age. Such dogs often seem to forget that they were housebroken and where their food bowls are, and they may even fail to recognize their owners.

A tremendous human-animal bonding relationship is established with all dogs, particularly senior dogs. This precious relationship deteriorates when the dog does not recognize his master. The drug can restore the bond and make senior dogs feel more like their "old selves."

ing, baring teeth, etc., can be frightening. It is important to ascertain why the dog is acting in this manner. Aggression is a display of dominance, and the dog should not have the dominant role in his pack, which is, in this case, your family.

It is important not to challenge an aggressive dog, as this could provoke an attack. Observe your Eskie's body language. Does he make direct eye contact and stare? Does he try to make himself as large as possible: ears pricked, chest out, tail erect? Height and size signify authority in a dog pack—being taller or "above" another dog literally means that he is "above" in social status. These body signals tell you that your Eskie thinks he is in charge, a problem that needs to be addressed. An aggressive dog is unpredictable; you never know when he is going to strike and what he is going to do. You cannot understand why a dog that is playful one minute is growling the next.

Fear is a common cause of aggression in dogs. Perhaps your Eskie had a negative experience as a puppy, which causes him to be fearful when a similar situation presents itself later in life. The dog may act aggressively in order to protect himself from whatever is making him afraid. It is not always easy to determine what is making your dog fearful, but if you can

> **TUG-OF-WAR**
> You should never play tug-of-war games with your puppy. Such games create a struggle for "top dog" position and teach the puppy that it is okay to challenge you. It will also encourage your puppy's natural tendency to bite down hard and *win*.

isolate what brings out the fear reaction, you can help the dog get over it.

Supervise your Eskie's interactions with people and other dogs, and praise the dog when it goes well. If he starts to act aggressively in a situation, correct him and remove him from the situation. Do not let people approach the dog and start petting him without your express permission. That way, you can have the dog sit to accept petting, and praise him when he behaves properly. You are focusing on praise and on modifying his behavior by rewarding him when he acts appropriately. By being gentle and by supervising his interactions, you are showing him that there is no need to be afraid or defensive.

The best solution is to consult a behavioral specialist, one who has experience with the American Eskimo Dog if possible. Together, perhaps you can pinpoint the cause of your dog's aggression and do something about it. An aggressive dog cannot be trusted, and a

> ### THE MIGHTY MALE
>
> Males, whether castrated or not, will mount almost anything: a pillow, your leg or, much to your dismay, even your neighbor's leg. As with other types of inappropriate behavior, the dog must be corrected while in the act, which for once is not difficult. Often he will not let go! While a puppy is experimenting with his very first urges, his owners feel he needs to "sow his oats" and allow the pup to mount. As the pup grows into a full-size dog, with full-size urges, it becomes a nuisance and an embarrassment. Males always appear as if they are trying to "save the race," more determined and stronger than imaginable. While altering the dog at an appropriate age will limit the dog's desire, it usually does not remove it entirely.

dog that cannot be trusted is not safe to have as a family pet. If, very unusually, you find that your pet has become untrustworthy and you feel it necessary to seek a new home with a more suitable family and environment, explain fully to the new owners all of your reasons for rehoming the dog to be fair to all concerned.

SEXUAL BEHAVIOR

Dogs exhibit certain sexual behaviors that may have influenced your choice of male or female when you first purchased your American Eskimo. To a certain extent, spaying/neutering will eliminate these behaviors, but if you are purchasing a dog that you wish to breed from, you should be aware of what you will have to deal with throughout the dog's life.

Female dogs usually have two estruses per year, with each season lasting about three weeks. These are the only times in which a female dog will mate, and she usually will not allow this until the second week of the cycle, although this varies from bitch to bitch. If not bred during the heat cycle, it is not uncommon for a bitch to experience a false pregnancy, in which her mammary glands swell and she exhibits maternal tendencies toward toys or other objects.

With male dogs, owners must be aware that whole dogs (dogs who are not neutered) have the natural inclination to mark their territory. Males mark their territory by spraying small amounts of urine as they lift their legs in a macho ritual. Marking can occur both outdoors in the yard and around the neighborhood as well as indoors on furniture legs, curtains and the sofa. Such behavior can be very frustrating for the owner; early training is strongly urged before the "urge" strikes your dog. Neutering the male at an appropriate early age can solve this problem before it becomes a habit.

Other problems associated

with males are wandering and mounting. Both of these habits, of course, belong to the unneutered dog, whose sexual drive leads him away from home in search of the bitch in heat. Males will mount females in heat, as well as any other dog, male or female, that happens to catch their fancy. Other possible mounting partners include his owner, the furniture, guests to the home and strangers on the street. Discourage such behavior early on.

Owners must further recognize that mounting is not merely a sexual expression but also one of dominance, seen in males and females alike. Be consistent and be persistent, and you will find that you can "move mounters."

CHEWING

The national canine pastime is chewing! Every dog loves to sink his "canines" into a tasty bone, so it is important to provide your dog with appropriate chew toys so that he doesn't destroy your possessions or make a habit of gnawing on your hands and fingers. Dogs need to chew to massage their gums, to make their new teeth feel better and to exercise their jaws. This is a natural behavior that is deeply embedded in all things canine. Our role as owners is not to stop the dog's chewing, but rather to redirect it to positive, chew-worthy objects. Be an informed owner and purchase proper chew toys, like strong nylon bones, that will not splinter.

A male's lifting his leg to mark territory is a normal canine behavior, but it can be surprising to owners what their dogs find suitable to mark!

Be sure that the objects are safe and durable, since your dog's safety is at risk. Again, the owner is responsible for ensuring a dog-proof environment.

The best answer is prevention; that is, put your shoes, handbags and other tasty objects in their proper places (out of the reach of the growing canine mouth). Direct your pup to his toys whenever you see him "tasting" the furniture legs or the leg of your trousers. Make a loud noise to attract the pup's attention and immediately escort him to his chew toy and engage him with the toy for at least four minutes, praising and encouraging him all the while. An array of safe, interesting chew toys will keep your dog's mind and teeth occupied, and keep him distracted from chewing on things he shouldn't.

Some trainers recommend deterrents, such as hot pepper, a bitter spice or a product designed for this purpose, to discourage the dog from chewing unwanted objects. Test these products to see which works best before investing in large quantities.

JUMPING UP
Jumping up is a dog's friendly way of saying hello! Some dog owners do not mind when their dog jumps up. The problem arises when guests come to the house and the dog greets them in the same manner—whether they like it or not! However friendly the greeting may be, the chances are that your visitors will not appreciate your dog's enthusiasm. The dog will not be able to distinguish upon whom he can jump and whom he cannot. Therefore, it is probably best to discourage this behavior entirely.

Pick a command such as "Off" (avoid using "Down" since you will use that for the dog to lie down) and tell him "Off" when he jumps up. Place him on the ground on all fours and have him sit, praising him the whole time. Always lavish him with praise and petting when he is in the sit position. In this way, you can give him a warm affectionate greeting, let him know that you are as excited to see him as he is to see you and instill good manners at the same time!

DIGGING
Digging, which is seen as a destructive behavior to humans, is actually quite a natural behavior in dogs. Although terriers (the "earth dogs") are most associated with the digging, any dog's desire to dig can be irrepressible and most frustrating to his owners. When digging occurs in your yard, it is actually a normal behavior redirected into something the dog can do in his everyday life. In the wild, a dog would be actively seeking food, making his own shelter, etc. He would be using his

paws in a purposeful manner for his survival. Since you provide him with food and shelter, he has no need to use his paws for these purposes, and so the energy that he would be using may manifest itself in the form of little holes all over your yard and flowerbeds.

Perhaps your dog is digging as a reaction to boredom—it is somewhat similar to someone eating a whole bag of chips in front of the TV—because they are there and there is nothing better to do! Basically, the answer is to provide the dog with adequate play and exercise so that his mind and paws are occupied, and so that he feels as if he is doing something useful.

Of course, digging is easiest to control if it is stopped as soon as possible, but it is often hard to catch a dog in the act. If your dog is a compulsive digger and is not easily distracted by other activities, you can designate an area on your property where he is allowed to dig. If you catch him digging in an off-limits area of the yard, immediately take him to the approved area and praise him for digging there. Keep a close eye on him so that you can catch him in the act—that is the only way to make him understand what is permitted and what is not. If you take him to a hole he dug an hour ago and tell him "No," he will understand that you are not fond of holes, dirt or flowers. If you

BARKING STANCE
Did you know that a dog is less likely to bark when sitting than standing? Watch your dog the next time that you suspect he is about to start barking. You'll notice that, as he does, he gets up on all four feet. Hence, when teaching a dog to stop barking, it helps to get him to sit before you command him to be quiet.

catch him while he is stifle-deep in your tulips, that is when he will get your message.

BARKING

Dogs cannot talk—oh, what they would say if they could! Instead, barking is a dog's way of "talking." It can be somewhat frustrating because it is not always easy to tell what a dog means by his bark—is he excited, happy, frightened or angry? Whatever it is that the dog is trying to say, he should not be punished for barking. It is only when the barking becomes excessive, and when the excessive barking becomes a bad habit, that the behavior needs to be modified.

Eskies tend to use their barks purposefully to "sound the alarm." If an intruder came into your home in the middle of the night and your Eskie barked a warning, wouldn't you be pleased? You would probably deem your dog a hero, a wonderful guardian and protector of the home. On the other hand, if a friend drops by unexpectedly, rings the doorbell and is greeted with a sudden sharp bark, you would probably be annoyed at the dog. But in reality, isn't this just the same behavior? The dog does not know any better. Unless he sees who is at the door and it is someone he knows, he will bark as a means of vocalizing that his (and your) territory is being threatened. While your friend is not posing a threat, it is all the same to the dog. Barking is his means of letting you know that there is an intrusion, whether friend or foe, on your property. This type of barking is instinctive and should not be discouraged.

Excessive habitual barking, however, is a problem that should be corrected early on, and Eskies can become nuisance barkers if not properly trained. As your Eskie grows up, you will be able to tell when his barking is purposeful and when it is for no reason. You will become able to distinguish your dog's different barks and their meanings. For example, the bark when someone comes to the door will be different than the bark when he is excited to see you. It is similar to a person's tone of voice, except that the dog has to rely totally on tone of voice because he does not have the benefit of using words. An incessant barker will be evident at an early age.

There are some things that encourage a dog to bark. For example, if your dog barks non-stop for a few minutes and you give him a treat to quiet him, he believes that you are rewarding him for barking. He will associate barking with getting a treat and will keep doing it until he is

---

DOG TALK

Deciphering your dog's barks is very similar to understanding a baby's cries: there is a different cry for eating, sleeping, potty needs, etc. Your dog talks to you not only through howls and groans but also through his body language. Baring teeth, staring and inflating the chest are all threatening gestures. If a dog greets you by licking his nose, turning his head or yawning, these are friendly, peacemaking gestures.

When a group of friends gets together, they just might have a noisy chat.

rewarded. On the other hand, if you give him a command such as "Quiet" and praise him after he has stopped barking for a few seconds, he will get the idea that being "quiet" is what you want him to do.

FOOD STEALING

Is your dog devising ways of stealing food from your coffee table or pantry? If so, you must answer the following questions: Is your Eskie a bit hungry, or is he "constantly famished" like many dogs seem to be? Face it, some dogs are more food-motivated than others. They are totally obsessed by the smell of food and can only think of their next meal. Food stealing is terrific fun and always yields a great reward—*food*, glorious food.

Your goal as an owner, therefore, is to be sensible about where food is placed in the home and to reprimand your dog whenever he is caught in the act of stealing. But remember, only reprimand your dog if you actually see him stealing, not later when the crime is discovered; that will be of no use at all and will only serve to confuse him.

BEGGING

Just like food stealing, begging is a favorite pastime of hungry puppies! It achieves that same terrific result—*food*! Dogs quickly learn that their owners keep the "good food" for ourselves, and that we humans do not dine on dry food alone. Begging is a conditioned

This dog's pen doesn't stop him from investigating, but it stops him from getting what's on the other side.

response related to a specific stimulus, time and place. The sounds of the kitchen—cans and bottles opening, crinkling bags, the smell of food in preparation, etc.—will excite the dog, and soon the paws will be in the air!

Here is the solution to stopping this behavior: Never give in to a beggar! You are rewarding the dog for sitting pretty, jumping up, whining and rubbing his nose into you by giving him food. By ignoring the dog, you will (eventually) force the behavior into extinction. Note that the behavior is likely to get worse before it disappears, so be sure there are not any "softies" in the family who will give in to little "Oliver" every time he whimpers, "More, please."

COPROPHAGIA

Feces eating is, to humans, one of the most disgusting behaviors that their dogs could engage in; yet, to dogs, it is perfectly normal. It is hard for us to understand why a dog would want to eat his own feces. He could be seeking certain nutrients that are missing from his diet, he could be just hungry or he could be attracted by the pleasing (to a dog) scent. While coprophagia most often refers to the dog's eating his own feces, a dog may just as likely eat that of another animal as well if he comes across it. Dogs often find the stool of cats and horses more palatable than that of other dogs.

Vets have found that diets with low levels of digestibility, containing relatively low levels of fiber and high levels of starch, increase coprophagia. Therefore, high-fiber diets may decrease the likelihood of dogs' eating feces. Both the consistency of the stool (how firm it feels in the dog's mouth) and the presence of undigested nutrients increase the likelihood. Once the dog develops diarrhea from feces eating, he will likely stop this distasteful habit.

To discourage this behavior, first make sure that the food you are feeding your dog is nutritionally complete and that he is getting enough food. If changes in his diet do not seem to work, and no medical cause can be found, you will have to modify the behavior through environmental control before it becomes a habit. The best way to prevent your dog from eating his stool is to make it unavailable—clean up after he eliminates and remove any stool from the yard. If it is not there, he cannot eat it.

Reprimanding for stool eating rarely impresses the dog. Vets recommend distracting the dog while he is in the act of stool eating. Coprophagia is seen most frequently in pups 6 to 12 months of age, and usually disappears around the dog's first birthday.

INDEX

My American Eskimo

PUT YOUR PUPPY'S FIRST PICTURE HERE

Dog's Name _____

Date _____ Photographer _____